THE SPECTACULAR SCIENCE OF THE HUMAN BODY

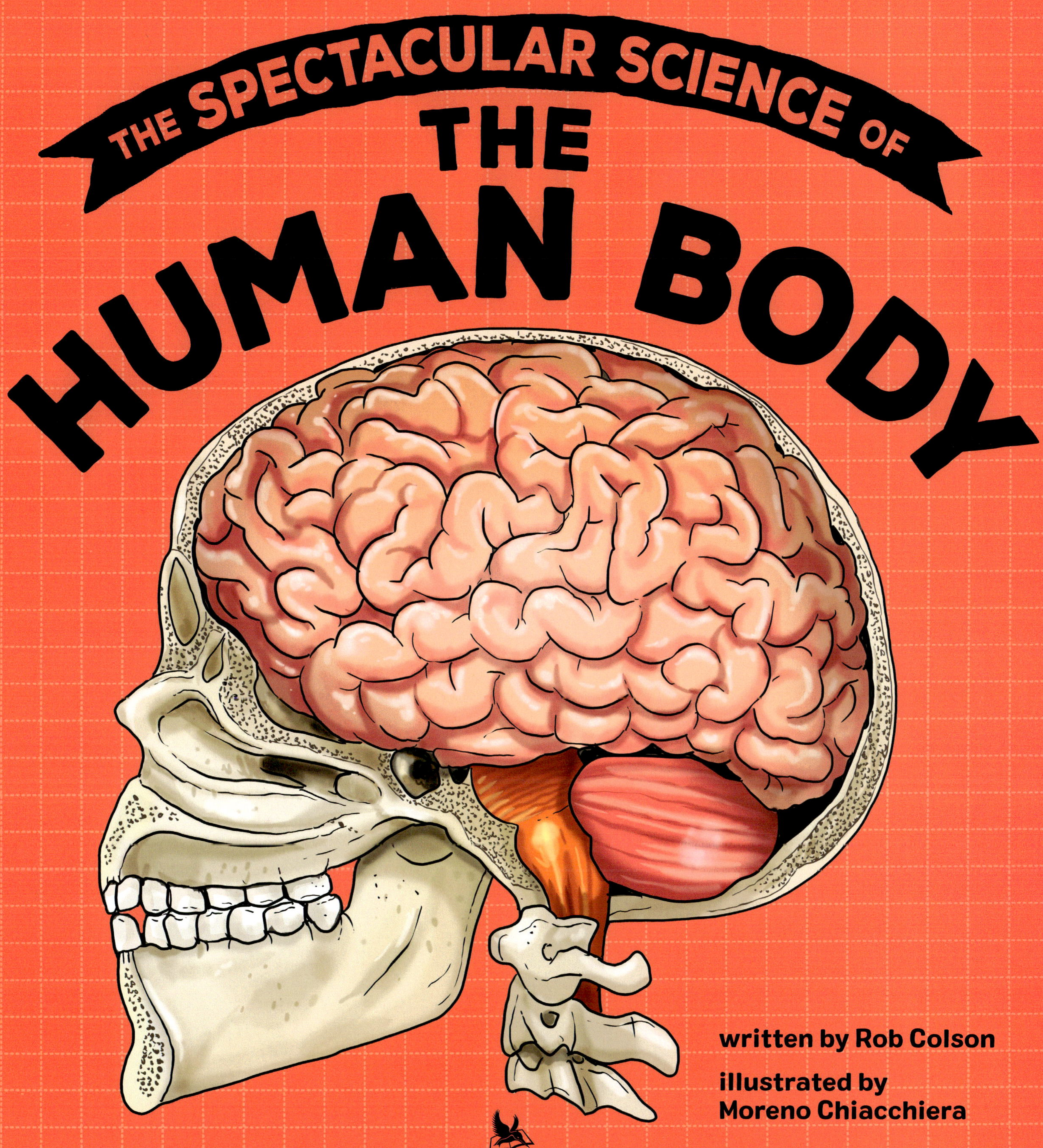

written by Rob Colson

illustrated by
Moreno Chiacchiera

KINGFISHER

First published 2023 by Kingfisher
an imprint of Macmillan Children's Books
The Smithson, 6 Briset Street,
London, EC1M 5NR
Associated companies
throughout the world
www.panmacmillan.com

EU representative: Macmillan Publishers
Ireland Limited, 1st Floor,
The Liffey Trust Centre, 117-126 Sheriff Street
Upper, Dublin 1, D01 YC43

Author: Rob Colson
Illustrator: Moreno Chiacchiera
Consultant: Nick Crumpton
Designed and edited by Tall Tree Ltd

ISBN: 978-0-7534-4866-3

A CIP catalogue record for this book is available from the British Library.

Printed in China
9 8 7 6 5 4 3 2 1
1TR/0823/WKT/RV/128MA

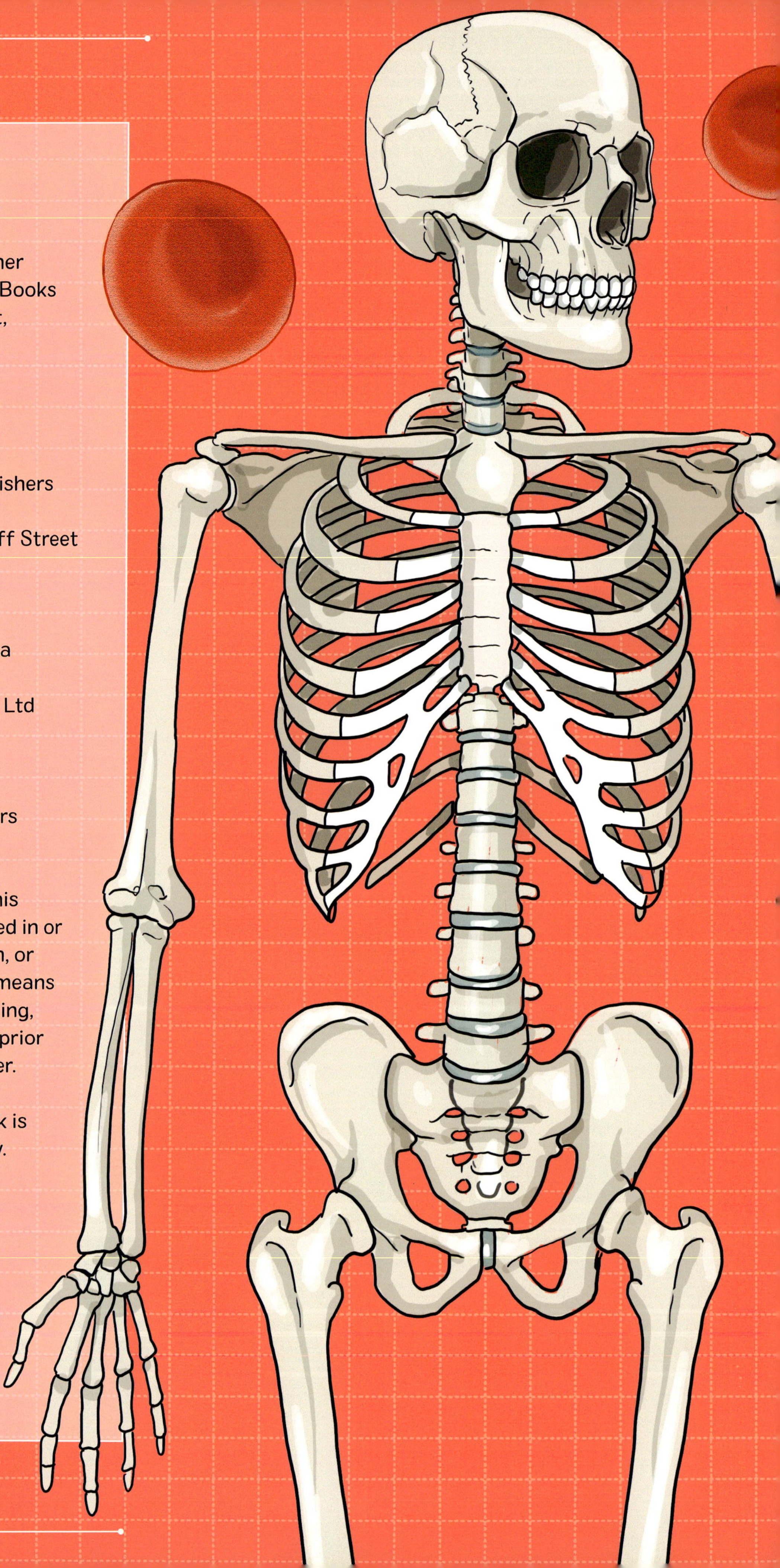

CONTENTS

A LIVING SYSTEM

Your body is a complex collection of different systems that work together to keep you alive.

CELLS

The smallest unit of the body is the cell (see pages 6–7). Cells can take a wide range of shapes and sizes, but most are so small that they cannot be seen by the naked eye.

Osteocyte (bone cell)

occupy small chambers within bones, surrounded by hard minerals.

Red blood cells

carry oxygen in the blood. They are made in bone marrow.

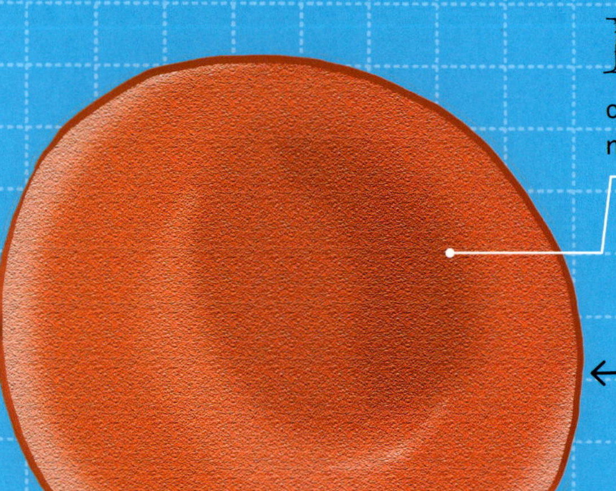

Red blood cell

Neurons

transmit messages around the body and within the brain.

Neuron (nerve cell)

TISSUES

Similar cells join together to form tissues. Connective tissue supports other tissue and binds them together. Connective tissues include bones, blood, tendons and ligaments. Epithelial tissue provides a protective covering. Epithelial tissues include the skin and the linings of tubes in the body. Muscle tissue is made of cells that can contract and makes up muscles. Nervous tissue is made from neurons and transmits messages.

The four main types of tissue

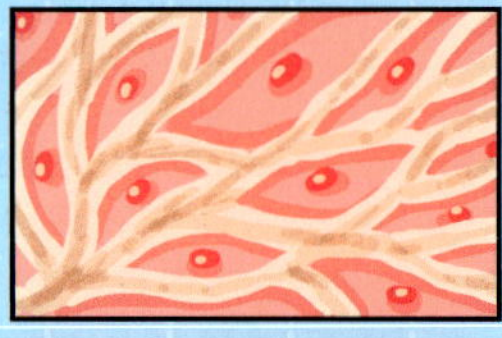

Connective tissue

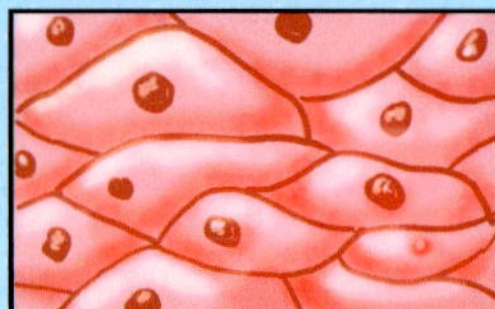

Epithelial tissue

Muscle tissue

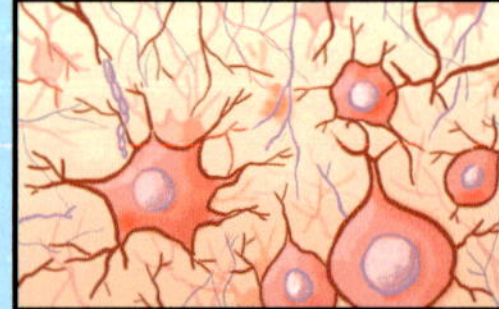

Nervous tissue

ORGANS

Tissues join together to form larger structures called organs. Organs carry out specific jobs in the body. For example, the heart pumps blood, while the stomach digests food. Organs work together in systems, and many organs take part in more than one system.

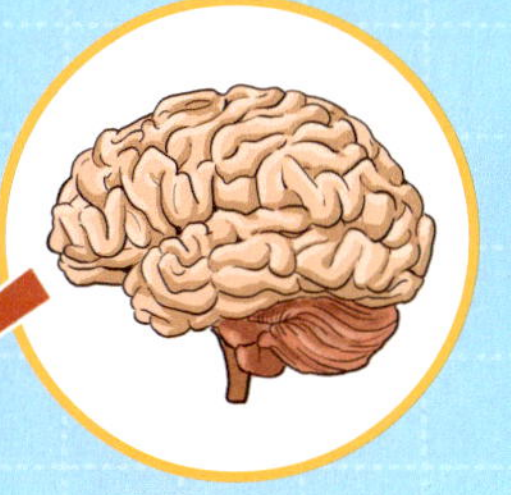

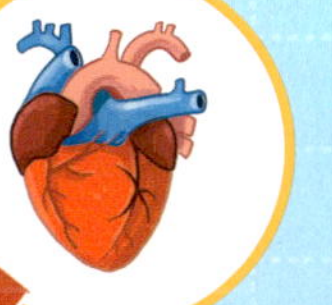

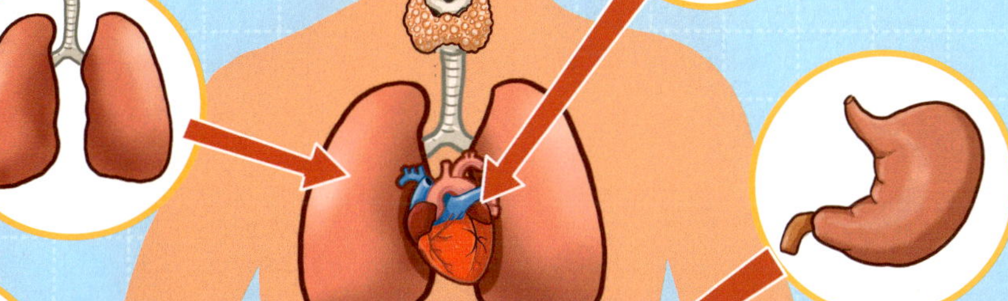

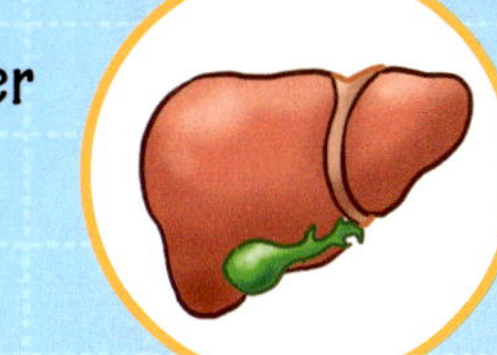

BODY AND MIND

Conscious minds are produced by the action of the brain as it works with the rest of the body. Our minds create a picture of ourselves in the world, and this allows us to plan ahead and make decisions. Staying conscious requires a lot of effort. Every day, we need to turn off our conscious minds for several hours when we sleep.

Scientists study sleep by measuring brain activity.

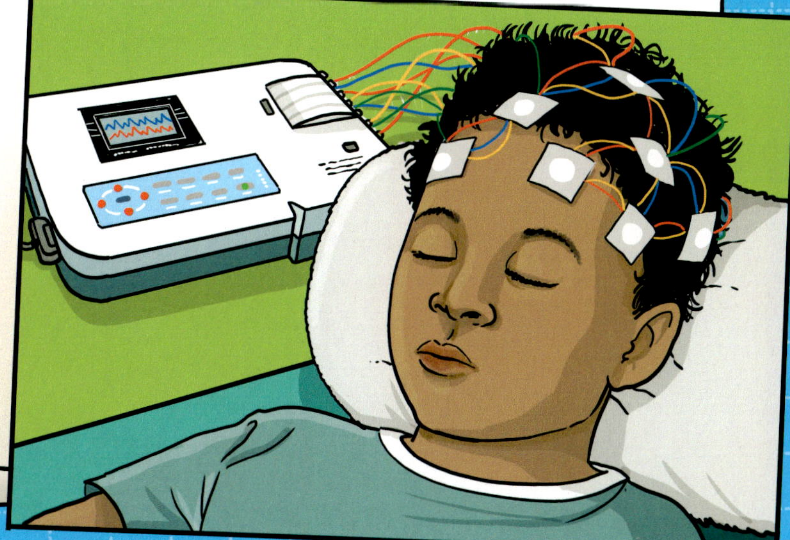

THE CELL

Your body is made of more than 30 trillion cells. Cells contain smaller parts called organelles, each of which has a different job to do. Each tiny cell is a complex living system of its own.

More than 1 million chemical reactions take place inside a cell every second!

Vacuoles store waste products.

STAYING BALANCED

Cells constantly monitor their internal state to keep the correct chemical balance. They take in just the right amount of nutrients from outside their cell wall to maintain a healthy mix of chemicals inside it. This process is called homeostasis.

Mitochondria

Most human cells contain mitochondria. These are the cells' energy packs. Mitochondria make a chemical called ATP (adenosine triphosphate). The ATP is sent around the cell to power all the different jobs it needs to do.

ANTONIE VAN LEEUWENHOEK

Dutch scientist Antonie van Leeuwenhoek (1632–1723) was one of the first people to study human cells using a microscope. He discovered sperm cells and gave an accurate description of the structure of red blood cells, which he described as '25,000 times smaller than a grain of sand'.

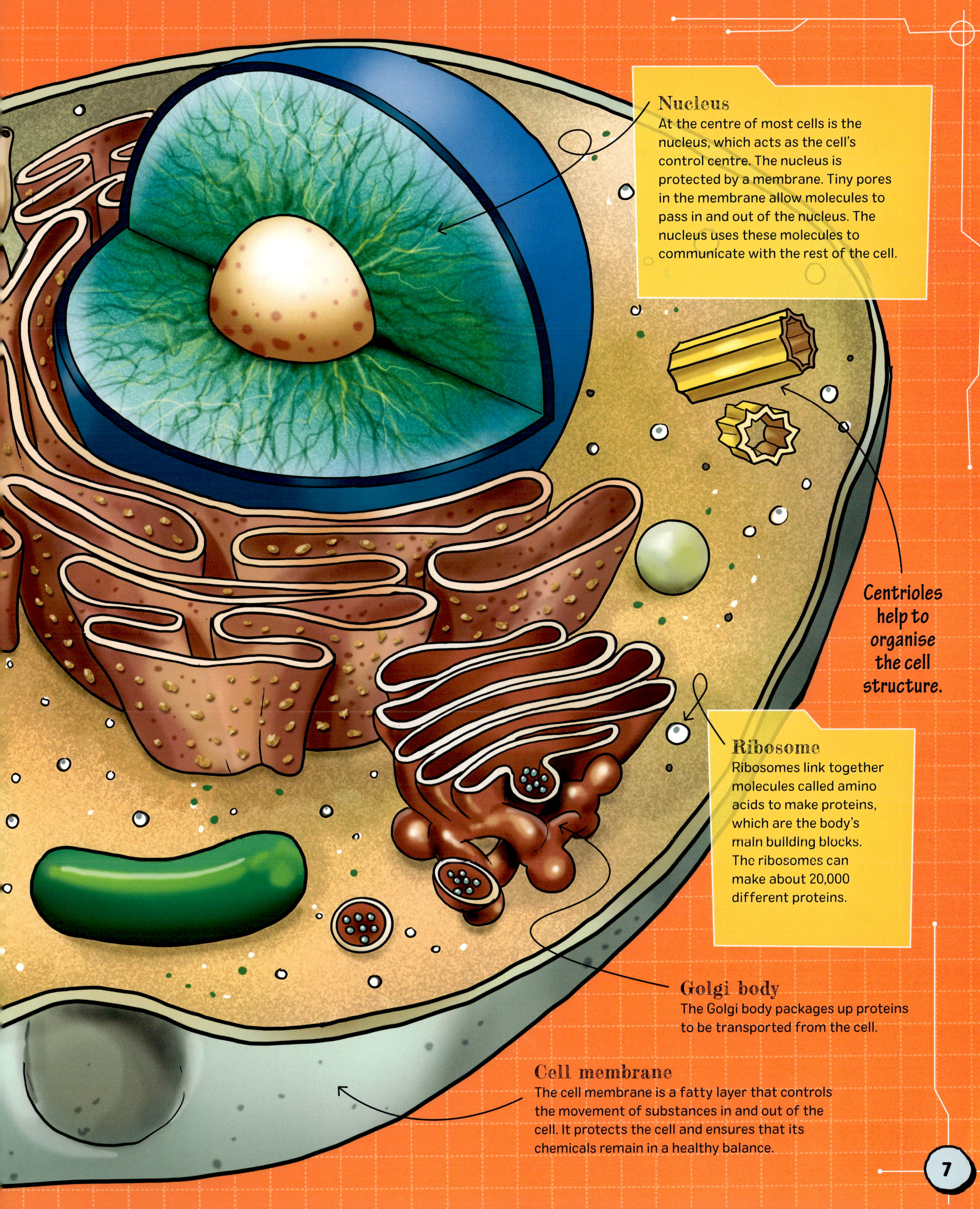
Nucleus
At the centre of most cells is the nucleus, which acts as the cell's control centre. The nucleus is protected by a membrane. Tiny pores in the membrane allow molecules to pass in and out of the nucleus. The nucleus uses these molecules to communicate with the rest of the cell.
Centrioles help to organise the cell structure.
Ribosome
Ribosomes link together molecules called amino acids to make proteins, which are the body's main building blocks. The ribosomes can make about 20,000 different proteins.
Golgi body
The Golgi body packages up proteins to be transported from the cell.
Cell membrane
The cell membrane is a fatty layer that controls the movement of substances in and out of the cell. It protects the cell and ensures that its chemicals remain in a healthy balance.

THE SKELETON

The skeleton is a system of about 206 bones. The bones are connected by joints (see pages 10–11) to give the body strength and protection and allow it to move.

STRUCTURE OF A BONE

Marrow
At the centre of a bone, a hollow shaft contains yellow bone marrow, which stores fat. Red bone marrow in spongy bone makes red blood cells.

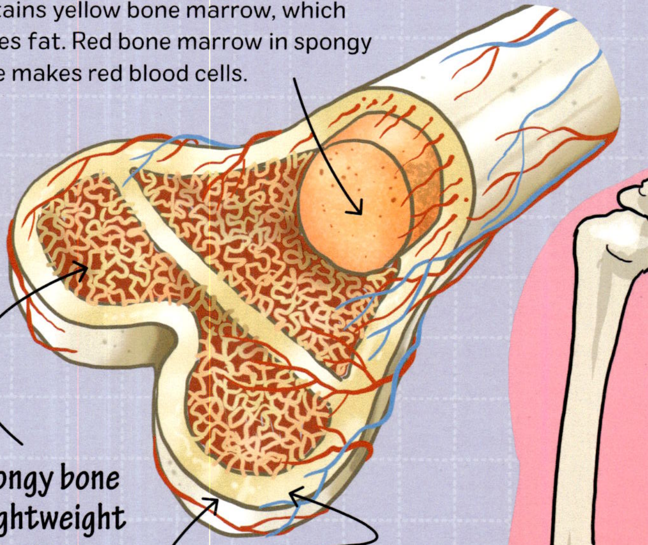

Spongy bone is lightweight but strong.

Compact bone gives the bone strength.

Periosteum
The periosteum is a thin outer membrane. It provides a blood supply to the bone.

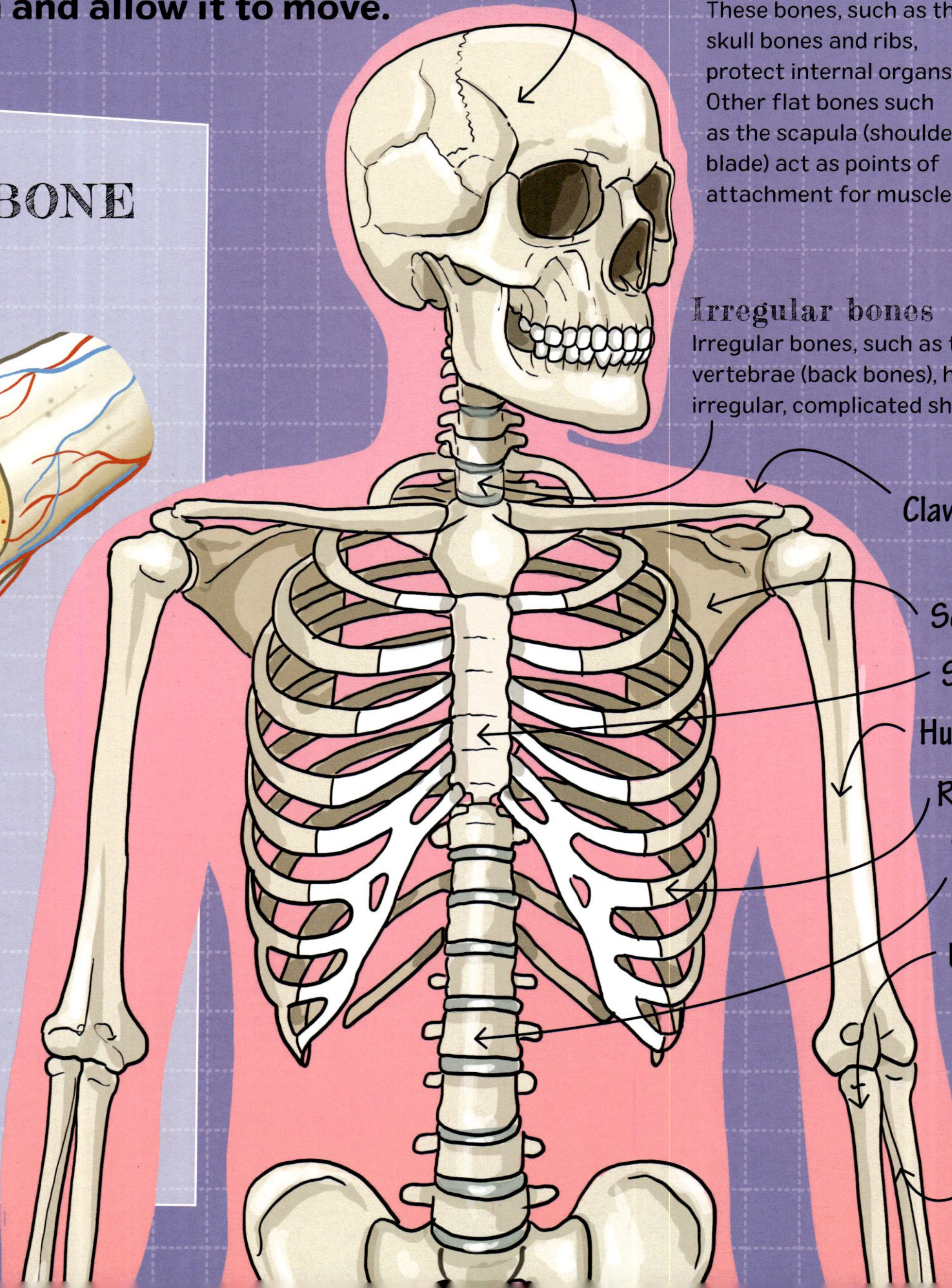

The axial skeleton (blue) forms the core of the body, protecting the vital organs.

Flat bones
Flat bones are thin bones with broad, flat surfaces. These bones, such as the skull bones and ribs, protect internal organs. Other flat bones such as the scapula (shoulder blade) act as points of attachment for muscles.

Irregular bones
Irregular bones, such as the vertebrae (back bones), have irregular, complicated shapes.

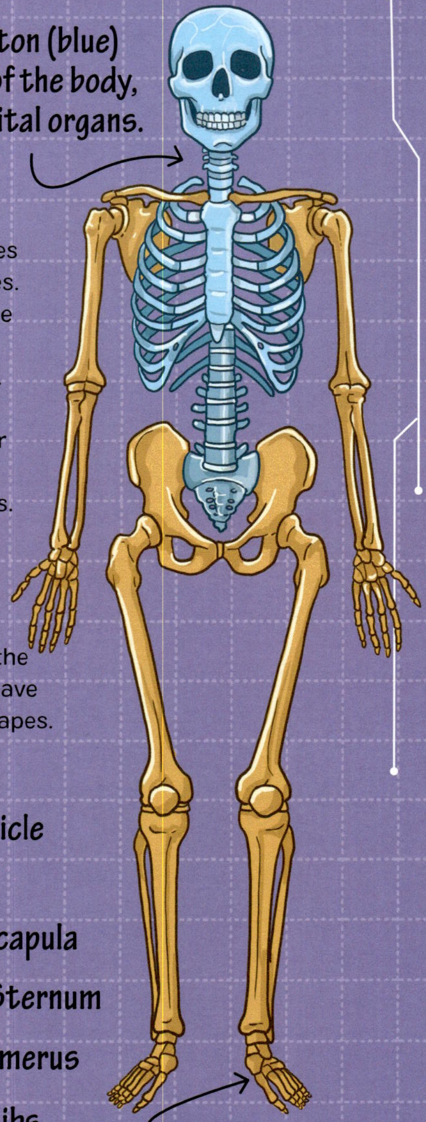

Clavicle

Scapula

Sternum

Humerus

Ribs

Vertebral column

Ulna

Radius

Ilium

The appendicular skeleton (yellow) forms the arms and legs.

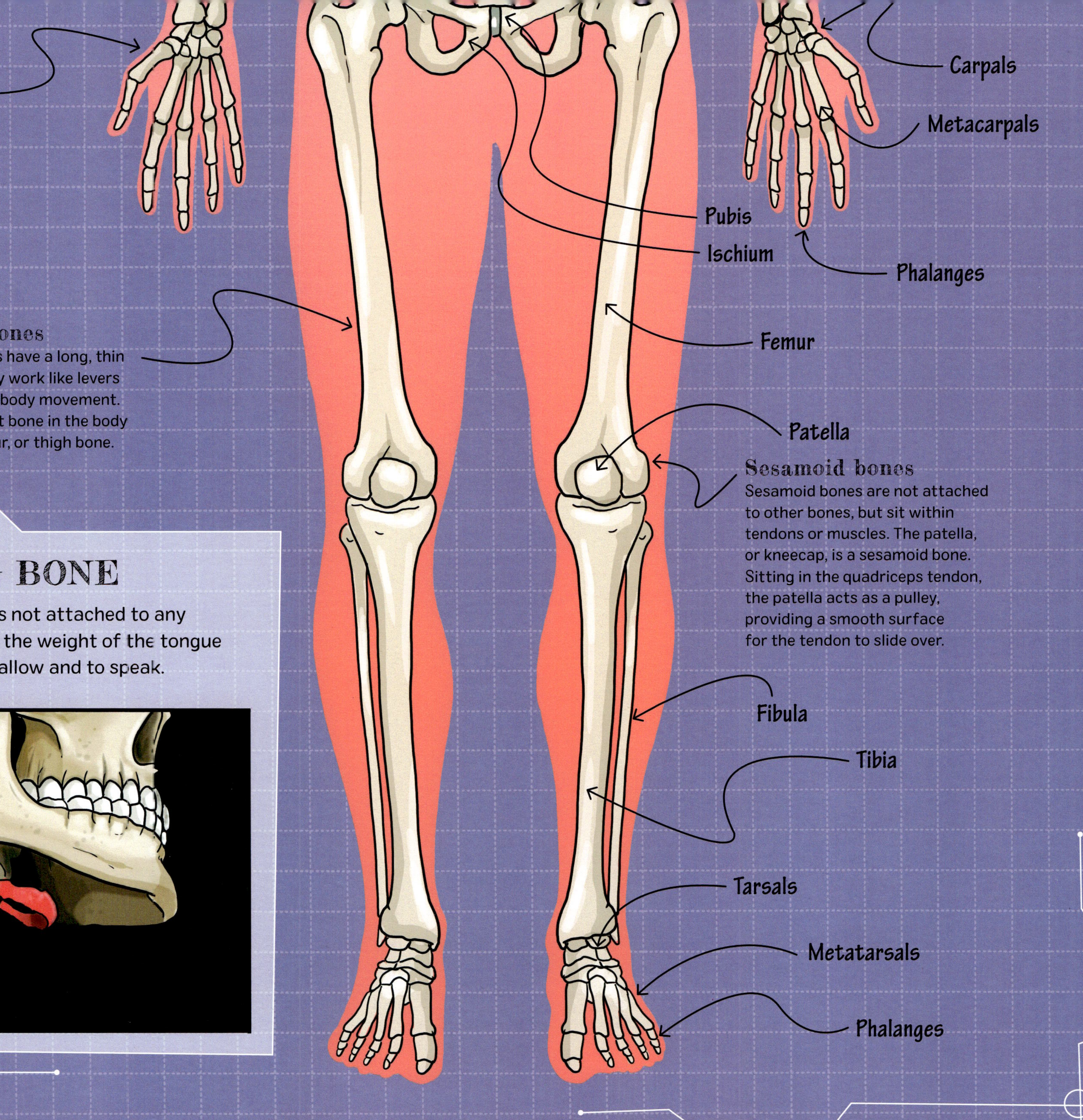

Short bones

Short bones are cube-shaped bones that are found in the wrist and ankles. They allow flexible movements of the hands and feet.

Long bones

Long bones have a long, thin shape. They work like levers to give the body movement. The longest bone in the body is the femur, or thigh bone.

Sesamoid bones

Sesamoid bones are not attached to other bones, but sit within tendons or muscles. The patella, or kneecap, is a sesamoid bone. Sitting in the quadriceps tendon, the patella acts as a pulley, providing a smooth surface for the tendon to slide over.

FLOATING BONE

The U-shaped hyoid is not attached to any other bone. It carries the weight of the tongue and allows you to swallow and to speak.

JOINTS

Bones meet at places called joints. Some joints allow lots of movement, while others hold the bones tightly in place.

Pivot joints

One bone rotates inside a ring created by a second bone. A pivot joint in your neck allows you to turn your head from side to side.

Ball-and-socket joints

The ball-shaped end of one bone sits inside the cup-shaped end of another. This allows movement in many different directions. Examples include the hips and shoulders.

Saddle joints

Two saddle-shaped ends of bones allow movement side to side and back and forth. The thumbs have saddle joints to allow lots of movement.

Ellipsoidal joints

The oval-shaped end of one bone sits inside an oval-shaped cup in a second bone. These are similar to ball-and-socket joints but have more restricted movement. They are found in the ankles and wrists.

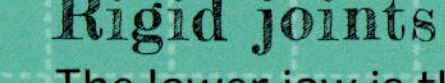

Rigid joints

The lower jaw is the only movable bone in the skull. The other 21 bones are fused together at rigid joints that don't allow movement.

Hinge joints

Like a door hinge, these joints only allow movement back and forth in one plane. Examples include the elbow, knee and finger joints.

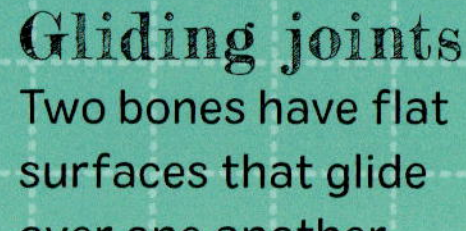

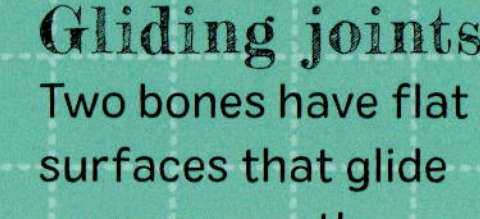

Gliding joints

Two bones have flat surfaces that glide over one another. These are found in the feet.

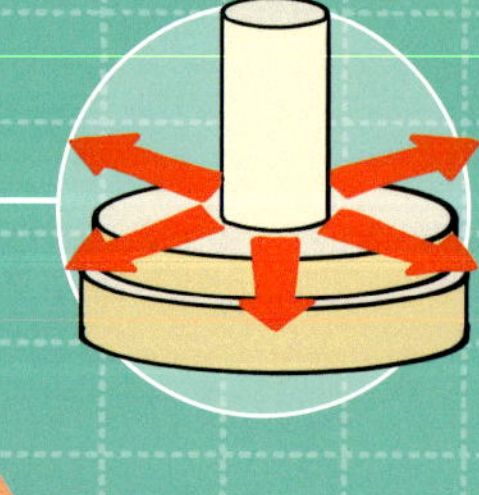

MUSCLES

Muscles move bones at joints. They also make the heart beat and push food through the digestive system.

MUSCLE TISSUES

There are three kinds of muscle tissue. Skeletal muscles move the bones. Cardiac muscle pumps blood around the heart. Smooth muscle lines the walls of organs such as the stomach. Muscle tissue can contract (become shorter) or relax.

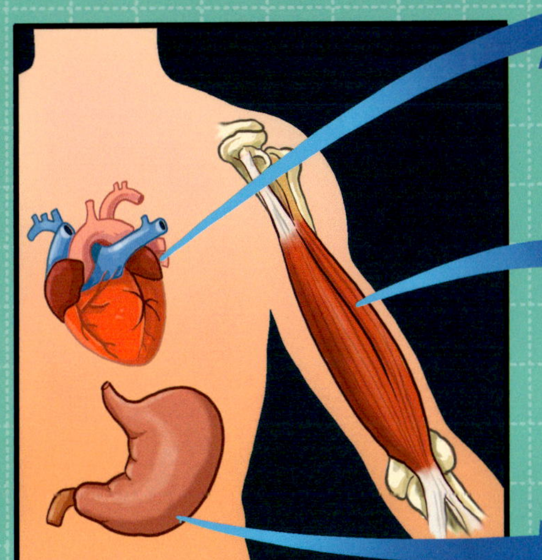

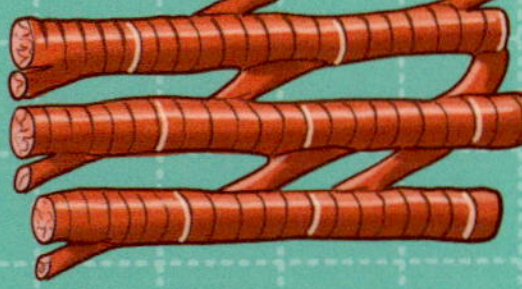

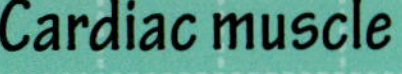

Cardiac muscle

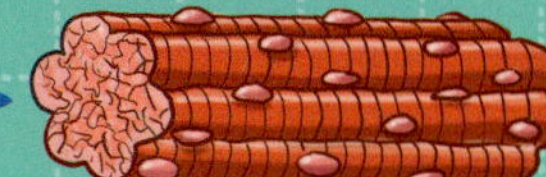

Skeletal muscle

Smooth muscle

PAIR WORK

Muscles work in pairs to move the bones. The biceps and triceps muscles work together to bend or straighten the arm.

To straighten the arm, the triceps contracts and the biceps relaxes.

Triceps

Biceps

To bend the arm, the biceps contracts and the triceps relaxes.

Sliding filaments

Muscles are made of bundles of long, cylindrical filaments. When a muscle relaxes, the thin filaments slide apart. When the muscle contracts, the thin filaments slide together.

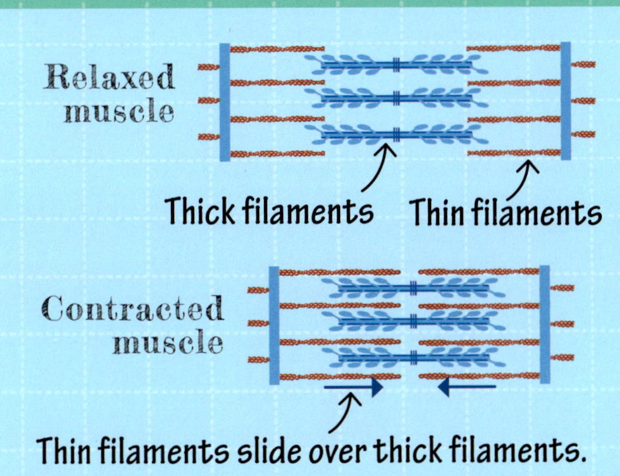

LUIGI AND LUCIA GALVANI

In 1780, Italian doctor Luigi Galvani (1737–1798) and his wife Lucia (1743–1788) made the muscles in a dead frog's legs twitch by applying an electric spark to them. Their experiment mimicked the way nerve cells use electricity to stimulate muscle fibres.

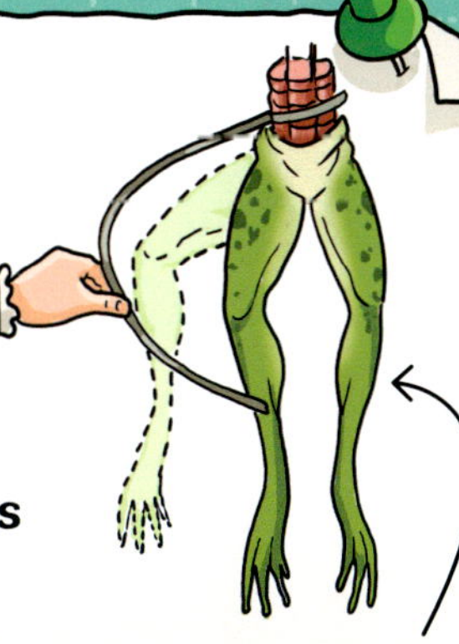

The dead frog's legs twitched when stimulated by electricity.

A PROTECTIVE BARRIER

The skin is the largest organ in the body. It helps us to control our temperature, prevents infection and acts as a barrier against the outside world. It is made of three layers.

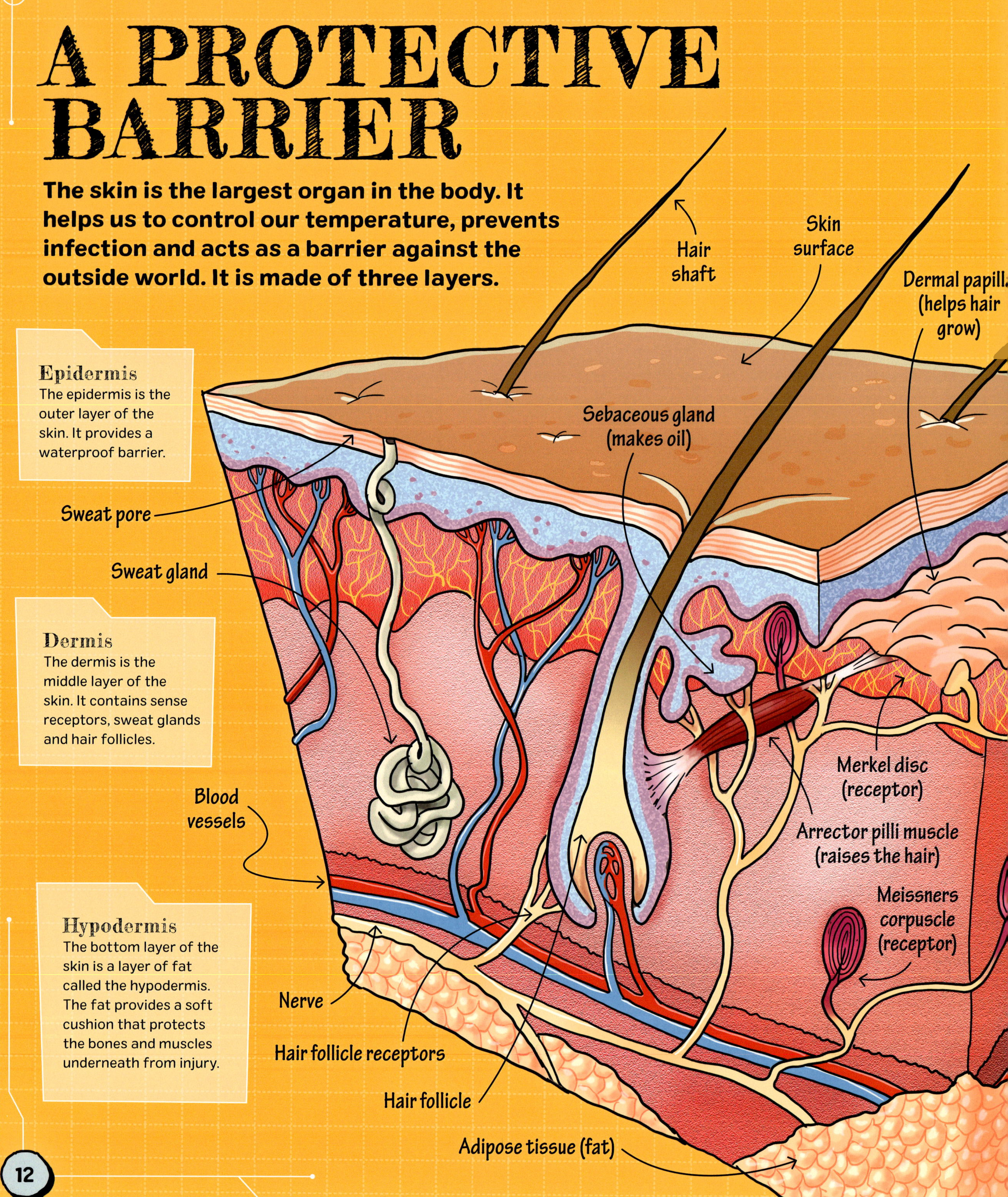

Epidermis

The epidermis is the outer layer of the skin. It provides a waterproof barrier.

Dermis

The dermis is the middle layer of the skin. It contains sense receptors, sweat glands and hair follicles.

Hypodermis

The bottom layer of the skin is a layer of fat called the hypodermis. The fat provides a soft cushion that protects the bones and muscles underneath from injury.

TEMPERATURE CONTROL

For our bodies to function properly, we need to maintain an internal temperature of 37°C.

When the body is in danger of overheating, blood is moved to the surface of the skin to lose heat. Sweat glands in the skin produce sweat, which evaporates from the surface of the skin. This evaporation also removes heat.

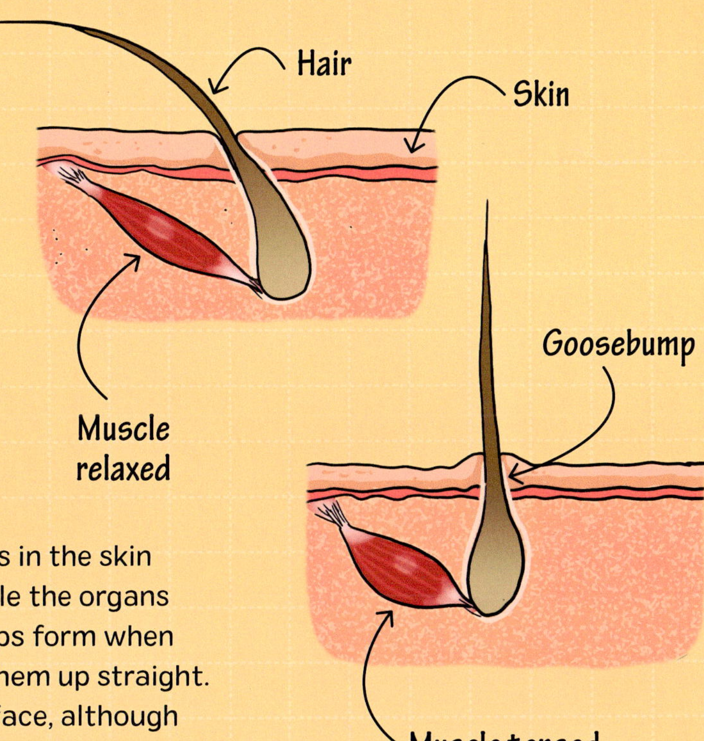

When the body is cold, blood vessels in the skin narrow. The skin becomes cold while the organs underneath stay warm. Goosebumps form when muscles at the base of hairs push them up straight. The erect hairs trap heat at the surface, although this works better for animals with thick fur!

SUNBURN

The sun's rays contain invisible ultraviolet light, which can burn the skin. Sunburn damages the dermis. To protect against burning, the skin produces a pigment called melanin in the epidermis. The melanin blocks much of the ultraviolet light. However, some still gets through, and it is very dangerous even in small amounts, so it is important to protect the skin by applying suncream.

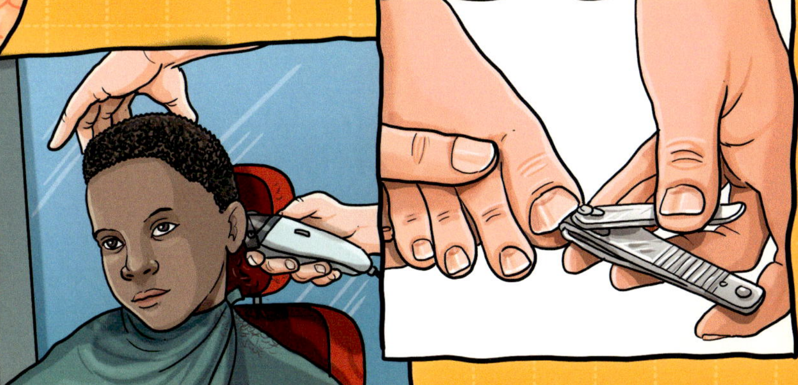

HAIR AND NAILS

Hair and nails contain a tough protein called keratin. Nails protect the tips of fingers and toes, while hair on your head keeps your head warm and protects it from sunburn. Hair and nails are made of dead cells, which is why it doesn't hurt when you cut them.

BODY BUGS

The skin is home to a range of micro-animals and microorganisms that are too small to see with the naked eye. Many of these organisms are harmless, but some cause diseases that need to be treated.

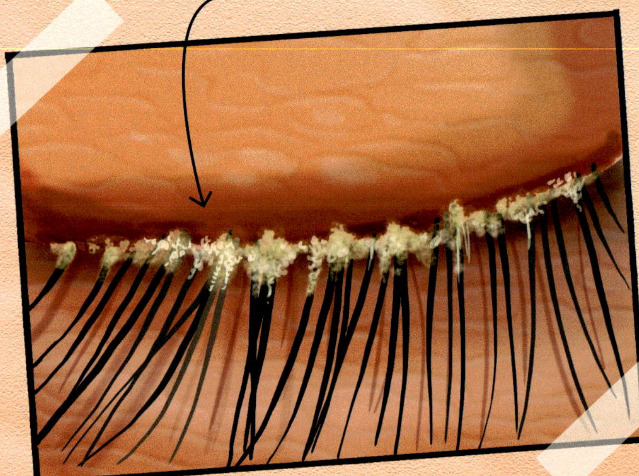

EYELASH MITES

Eyelash mites (scientific name *Demodex*) are tiny creatures that live on hair follicles, feeding on hair cells and oils in the skin. The mites are related to spiders. They have eight legs, which they use to cling on to hairs. They measure just 0.3 millimetres long and are often found in bunches at the base of eyelashes. The mites are usually harmless and most people have eyelash mites living on them without even realising it.

BELLYBUTTON BACTERIA

The bellybutton is an ideal breeding ground for bacteria, fungi and other microorganisms. More than 2,300 different kinds of bacteria have been found growing in people's bellybuttons, including the same bacteria that chefs use to make cheese!

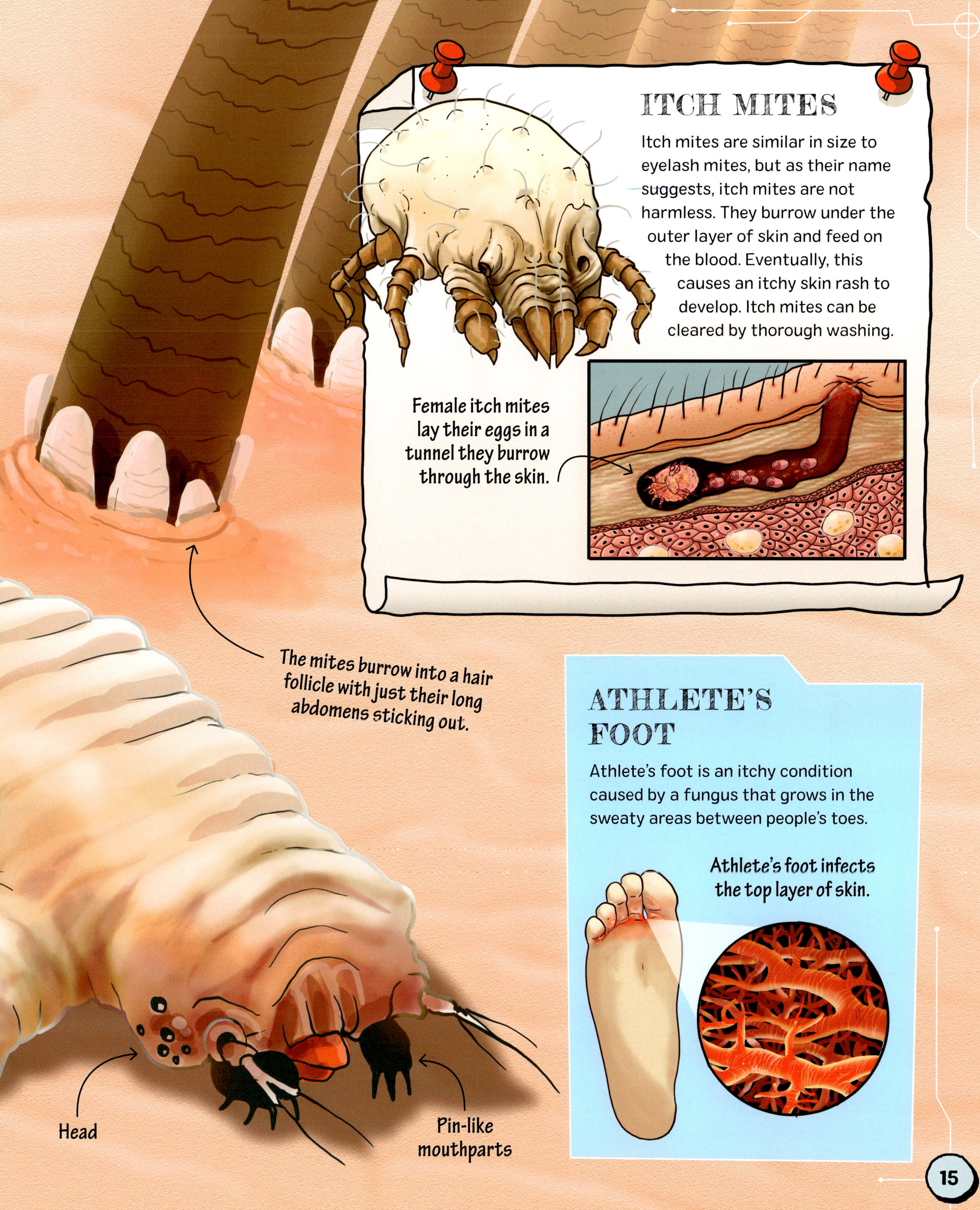
ITCH MITES
Itch mites are similar in size to eyelash mites, but as their name suggests, itch mites are not harmless. They burrow under the outer layer of skin and feed on the blood. Eventually, this causes an itchy skin rash to develop. Itch mites can be cleared by thorough washing.
Female itch mites lay their eggs in a tunnel they burrow through the skin.
The mites burrow into a hair follicle with just their long abdomens sticking out.
ATHLETE'S FOOT
Athlete's foot is an itchy condition caused by a fungus that grows in the sweaty areas between people's toes.
Athlete's foot infects the top layer of skin.
Head
Pin-like mouthparts

THE CIRCULATORY SYSTEM

The circulatory system pumps blood around the body. The blood carries nutrients and oxygen to cells and takes away waste products. The system is powered by a constantly beating muscle – the heart.

Superior vena cava (vein)
Aorta (artery)
Pulmonary artery (to lungs)
Pulmonary vein (from lungs)
Right atrium
Left atrium
Valves
Inferior vena cava (vein)
Right ventricle
Left ventricle

FOUR CHAMBERS

The heart is divided into four chambers: two upper atria and two lower ventricles. The two chambers on the right-hand side receive blood from the body's cells and pump it to the lungs. The two chambers on the left-hand side receive blood from the lungs and pump it to the cells.

Your heart beats about

once per second

Each heartbeat follows the same cycle.

HOW A HEART BEATS

1 The walls of the atria and ventricles relax, allowing blood to flow into the heart from the veins.

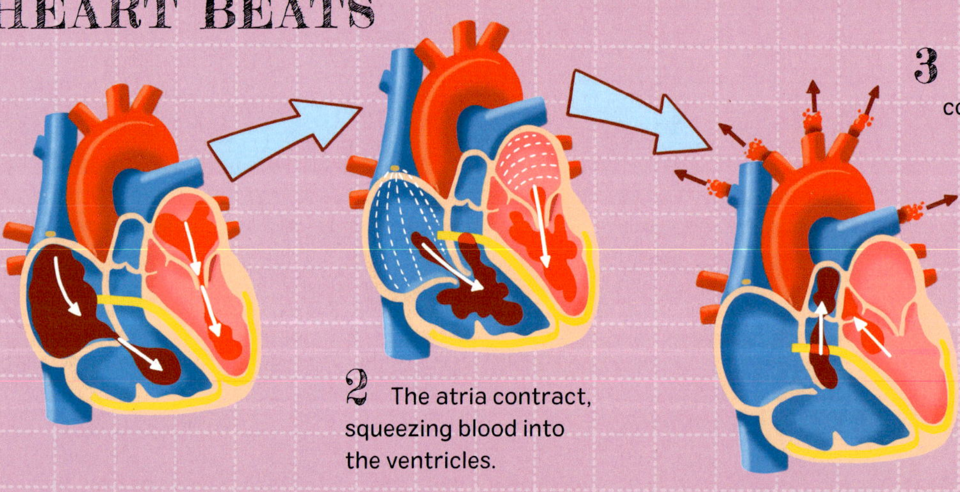

2 The atria contract, squeezing blood into the ventricles.

3 The walls of the ventricles contract. This squeezes blood into the arteries. A valve between the ventricles and the atria closes at this point to stop blood from flowing back into the atria. The right ventricle pumps blood to the lungs, while the left ventricle pumps blood around the body.

CIRCULATION

Blood flows around the body through a network of blood vessels. The heart pumps blood to the lungs, where the blood is filled with oxygen. The oxygenated blood then passes back to the heart. This is called the pulmonary circulation. The heart pumps the oxygenated blood around the body in the systemic circulation.

Capillaries are tiny blood vessels with thin walls that allow oxygen and nutrients to pass into cells.

Arteries carry blood away from the heart to the capillaries.

Veins carry blood from the capillaries back to the heart.

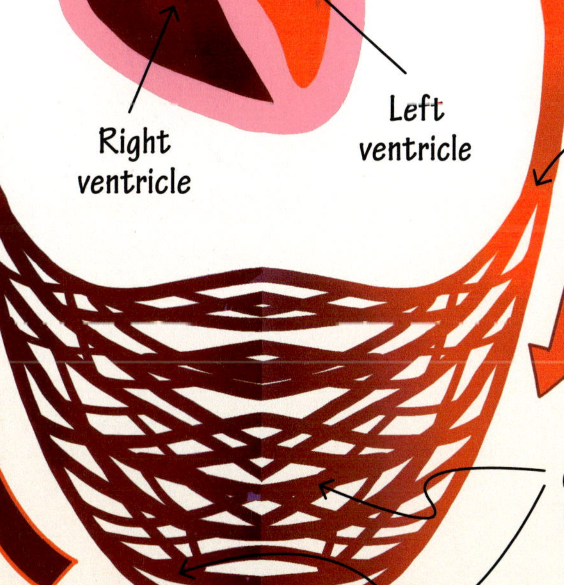

William Harvey

The circulation of blood was first described by English doctor William Harvey (1578–1657). Harvey showed that the purple blood in veins and the red blood in arteries were part of the same system, not two separate systems as previously thought.

THE NERVOUS SYSTEM

The nervous system carries signals to and from the brain and spinal cord. It is made up of billions of neurons, or nerve cells.

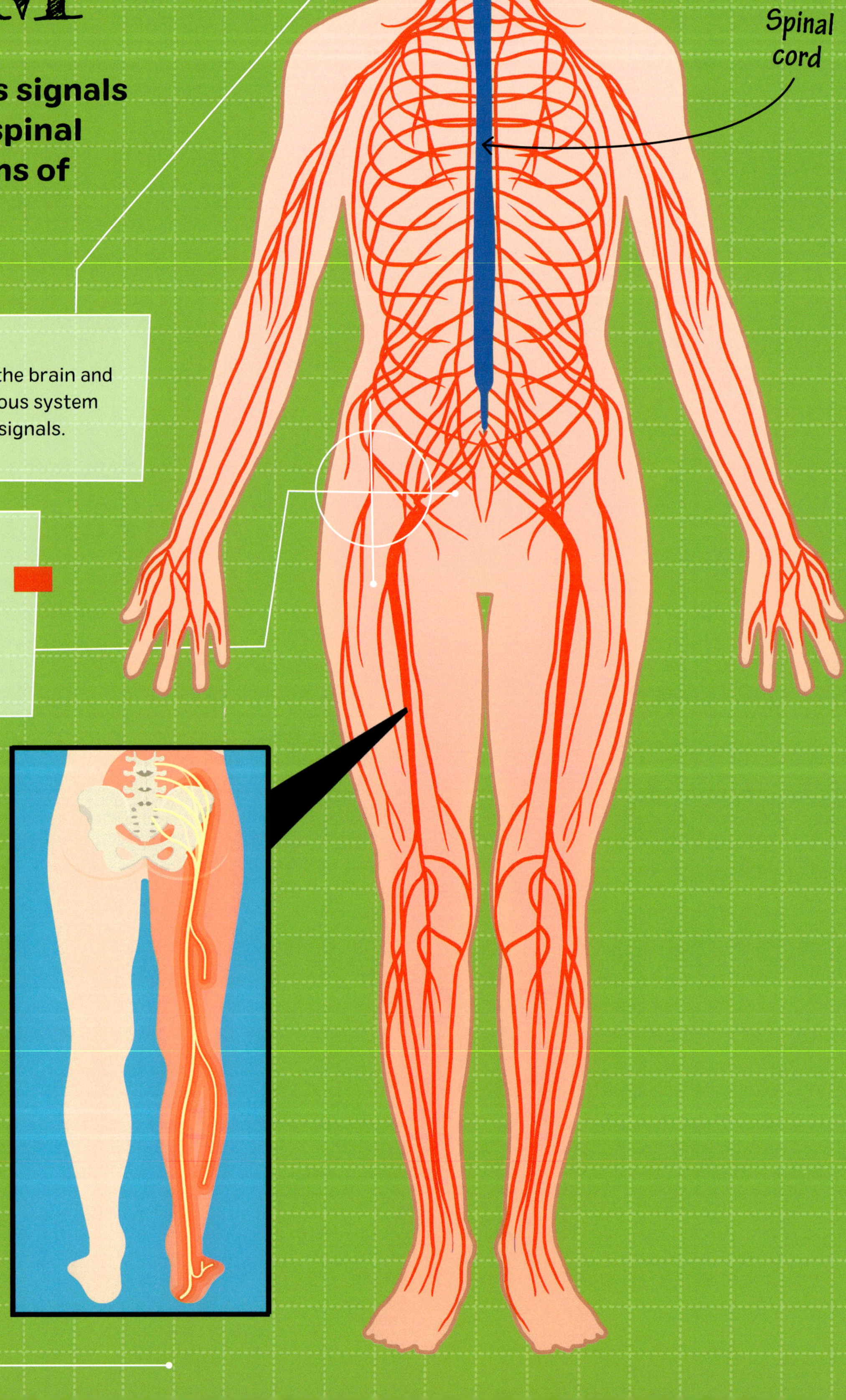

Central

The central nervous system is made up of the brain and the spinal cord. This is the part of the nervous system that processes information and sends out signals.

Peripheral

The peripheral nervous system relays information between the central nervous system and the rest of the body.

The longest neurons

in the body are found in the sciatic nerve, which runs from the bottom of the spinal cord to the foot. In tall people, the sciatic nerve can be 1 metre long. It allows you to feel sensations in your feet and lower leg and controls the muscles that move them.

NEURONS

Neurons both send and receive electrical signals. They send out their signal along a long, thin axon. They receive signals from other neurons through branching dendrites.

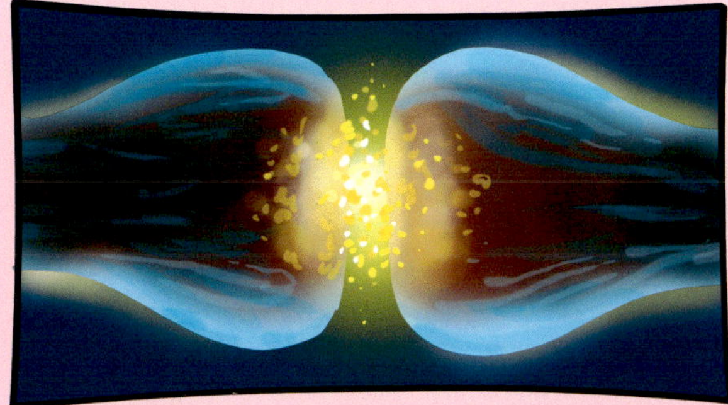

Synapse

The axon of one neuron meets the dendrite of another at a synapse. The neurons do not quite touch each other. Instead, the axon sends a signal to the dendrite by releasing chemicals across a tiny gap.

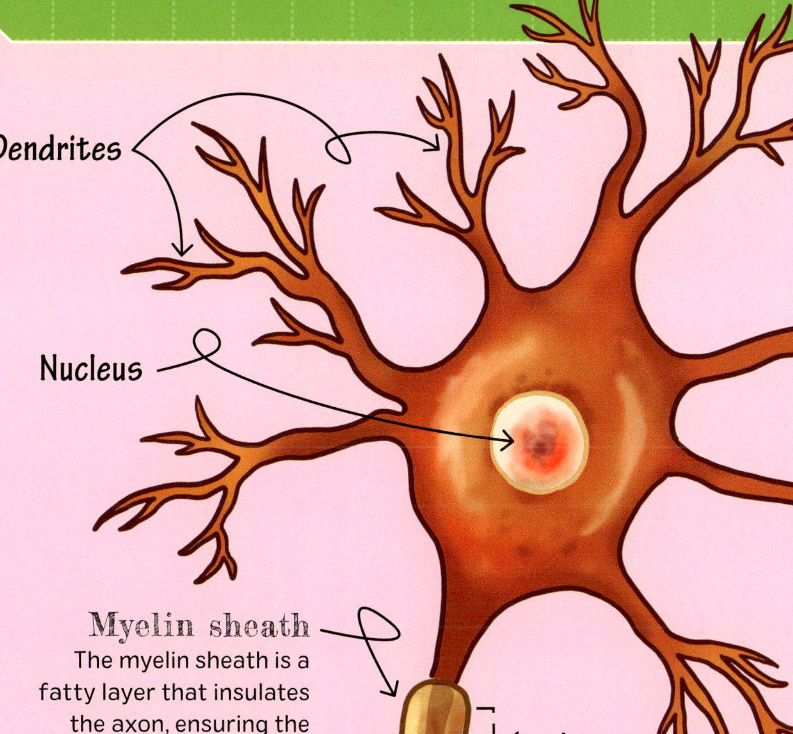

Myelin sheath

The myelin sheath is a fatty layer that insulates the axon, ensuring the electrical signal is sent quickly and efficiently.

Reaction times

Neurons send signals at up to 120 metres per second. When athletes hear the gun at the start of a race, it takes their brains at least 80 milliseconds to hear the sound and send a signal to their muscles to move. This is known as the reaction time. If an athlete reacts more quickly than this, they have made a false start.

REFLEXES

Some reactions don't involve the brain. Instead, the spinal cord sends a signal to muscles to react. The knee jerk reflex is caused by a tap on a spot below the knee cap. The spinal cord sends a signal to the thigh muscle to contract, kicking the foot up. This reaction takes just 50 milliseconds to happen.

Spinal cord

Receptor

Muscle

Leg jerks up when knee is tapped.

THE BRAIN

The brain contains about 85 billion neurons. Each neuron is connected to up to 10,000 other neurons, forming an ever-changing network of connections. Every second, your brain is constantly rewiring this network as it responds to the world.

PROTECTED ORGAN

The brain is about the size of a grapefruit. It is soft and squishy, a little like a blob of jelly, and it is easily damaged. For this reason, the brain is well protected inside the skull.

Cerebrum

The cerebrum is the largest part of the brain. It is covered by the cerebral cortex, which is a thin layer between 1 and 4 millimetres thick. The cortex is highly folded. This is the part of the brain that is responsible for processing information from the senses and problem-solving.

Cerebellum

The cerebellum (meaning 'little brain') sits at the back of the head. It coordinates muscle movements and maintains balance.

Brainstem

The brainstem connects the cerebrum to the spinal cord and controls many of the body's unconscious functions, such as heart rate.

Corpus callosum

The cerebrum and cerebellum are divided into two hemispheres. The hemispheres of the cerebrum are connected by the corpus callosum, which allows them to communicate with one another.

CORTEX FUNCTIONS

Different parts of the cortex are involved in different jobs, such as processing information from the senses. Each of these sections is found on both hemispheres of the brain. One section may have several jobs.

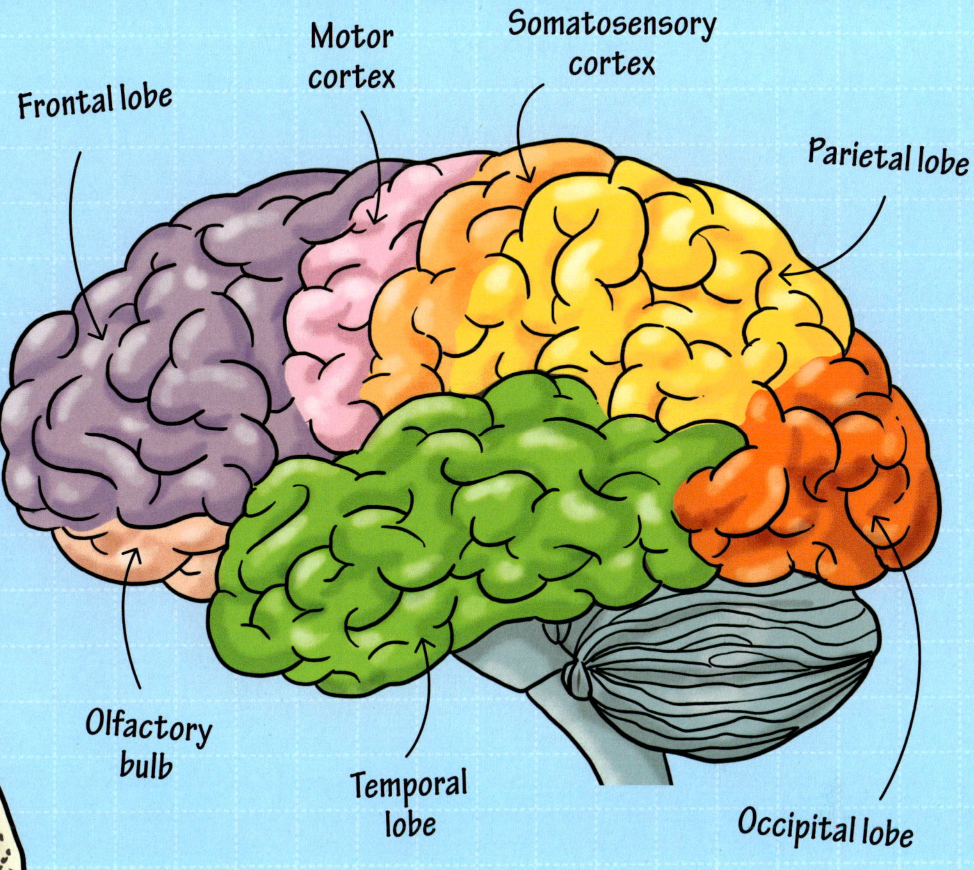

Frontal lobe performs many higher functions, allowing you to plan complex tasks using information from the whole of the brain.

Motor cortex controls movements. Body parts with fine movement control, such as the hands, have the most neurons dedicated to them.

Somatosensory cortex processes sensory information from across the body, including touch, temperature and pain.

Parietal lobe processes input from many different senses and helps to give you a sense of where you are in the world.

Occipital lobe processes vision. It gives depth and colour perception and facial recognition, and is also involved in memory formation.

Temporal lobe processes hearing. It is also involved in understanding language and laying down memories.

Olfactory bulb sits above the nose and processes the sense of smell.

VISION

Vision is one of the most important senses for humans. The information from our eyes allows our brains to form an image of the world around us.

BLIND SPOT

The point on the retina to which the optic nerve is connected cannot detect light. This causes a hole in the visual field called the blind spot. We do not normally notice our blind spots as our brains fill in the hole with a guess as to what is there.

OPTIC NERVE

The optic nerve carries information to an area at the back of the brain called the visual cortex. Signals from the left eye are sent to the right visual cortex. Signals from the right eye are sent to the left visual cortex.

RETINA

The retina is a light-sensitive tissue at the back of the eye. Special sensors called photoreceptors turn the light into electrical signals, which are sent to the brain through the optic nerve. The image on the retina is upside-down. The brain turns the image the right way up again.

RODS AND CONES

The retina contains two kinds of photoreceptors. Rods see images in black-and-white and allow you to see in low light levels. Cones are responsible for colour vision. There are three kinds of cone, each sensitive to different wavelengths of light: 60% of the cones sense the colour red, which has the longest wavelength; 30% of the cones sense green; and 10% of the cones sense blue, which has the shortest wavelength.

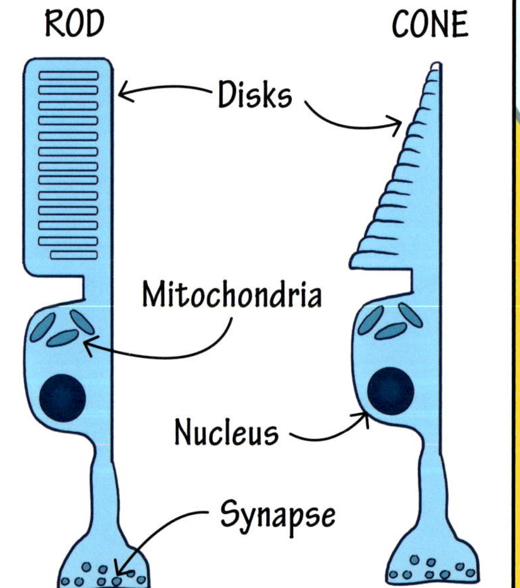

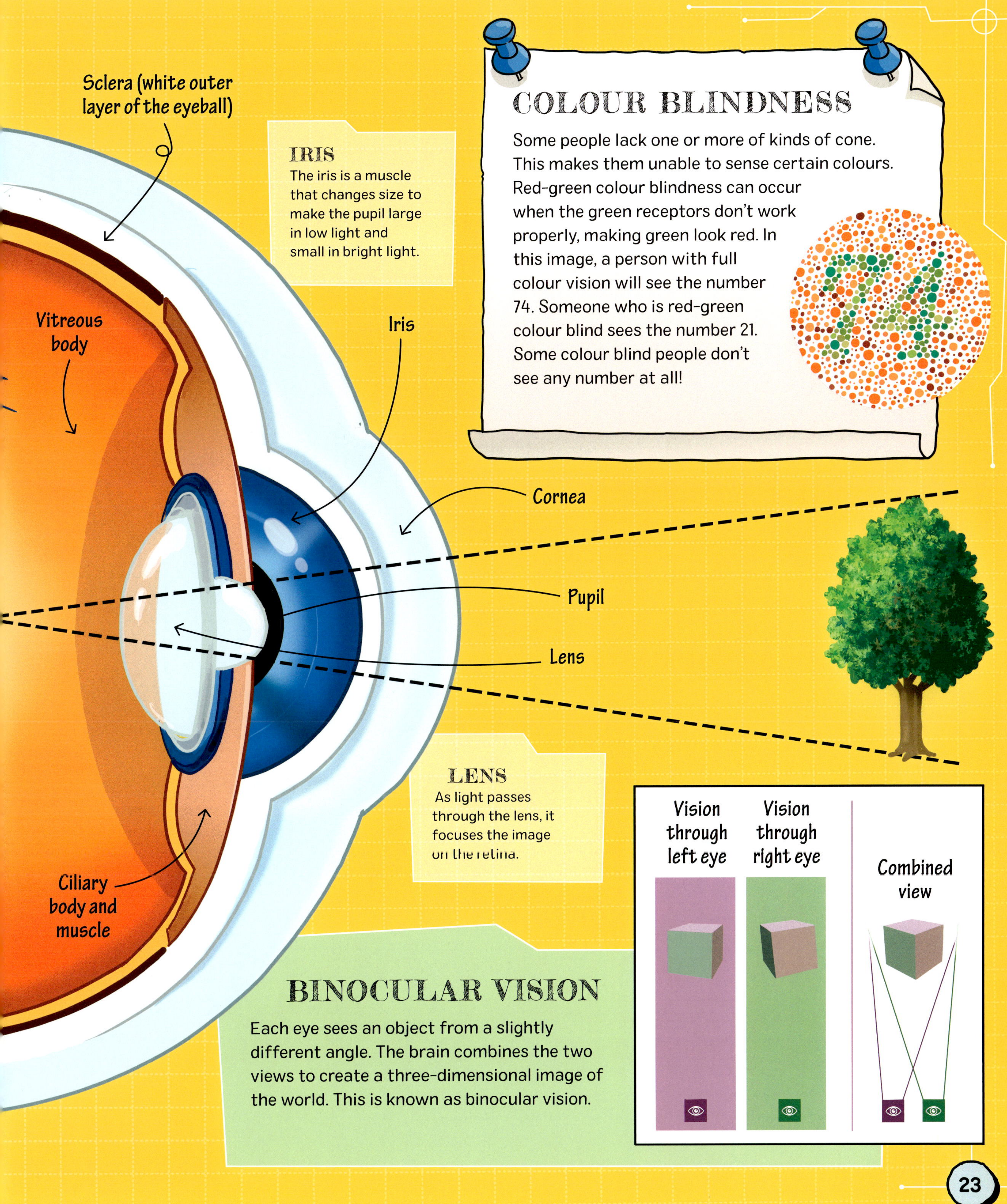

Sclera (white outer layer of the eyeball)
IRIS
The iris is a muscle that changes size to make the pupil large in low light and small in bright light.
COLOUR BLINDNESS
Some people lack one or more of kinds of cone. This makes them unable to sense certain colours. Red-green colour blindness can occur when the green receptors don't work properly, making green look red. In this image, a person with full colour vision will see the number 74. Someone who is red-green colour blind sees the number 21. Some colour blind people don't see any number at all!
Vitreous body
Iris
Cornea
Pupil
Lens
LENS
As light passes through the lens, it focuses the image on the retina.
Ciliary body and muscle
Vision through left eye
Vision through right eye
Combined view
BINOCULAR VISION
Each eye sees an object from a slightly different angle. The brain combines the two views to create a three-dimensional image of the world. This is known as binocular vision.

HEARING

The ears sense vibrations in the air. We hear these vibrations as sounds.

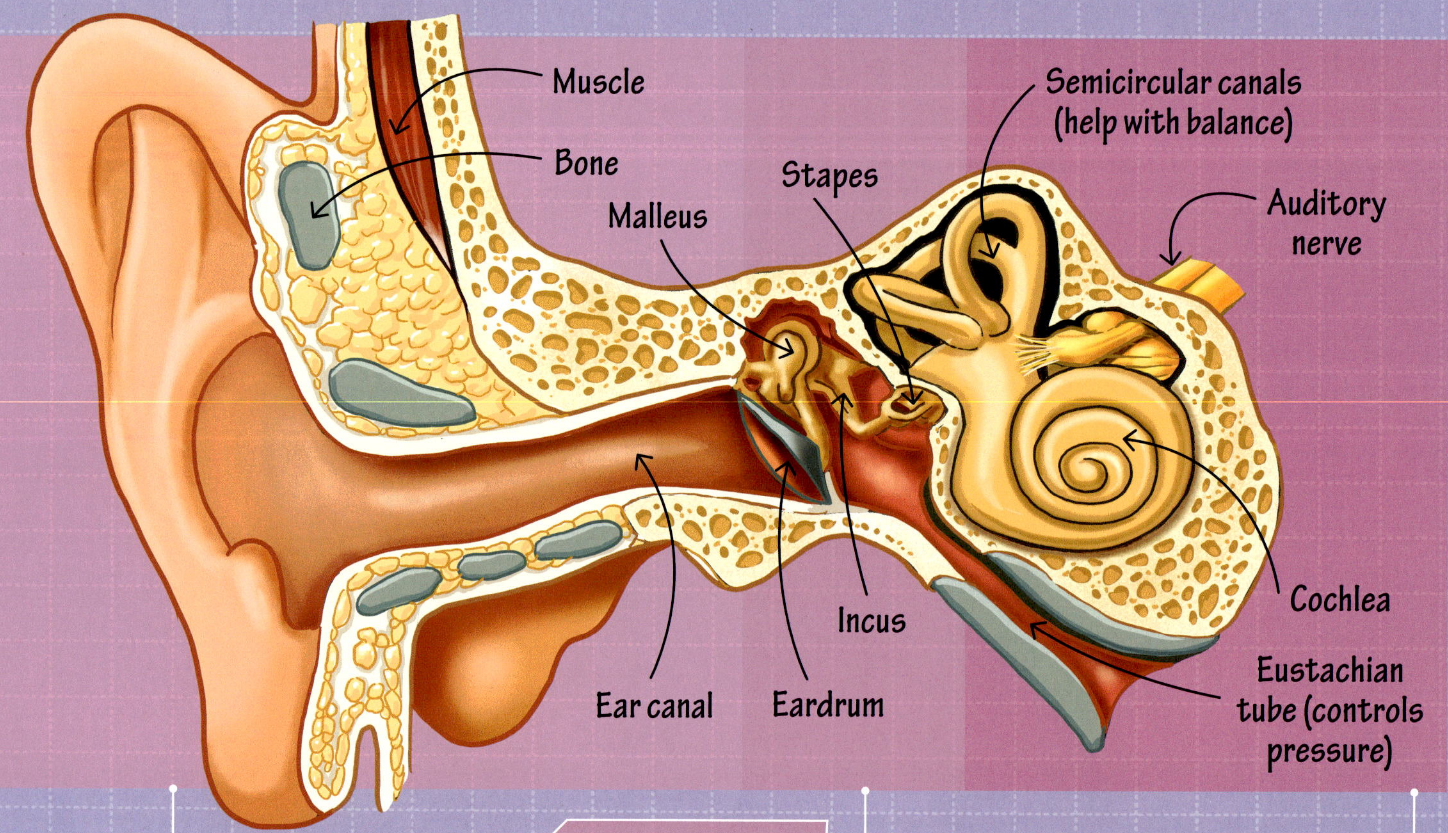

Outer ear

The outer ear channels sound waves through the ear canal.

Middle ear

At the end of the ear canal is a thin membrane called the tympanic membrane, or eardrum. Sounds cause the eardrum to vibrate. The vibrations are passed along three tiny bones in the middle ear called the ossicles (malleus, incus and stapes). The ossicles amplify the vibrations.

Inner ear

The ossicles pass the vibrations on to the spiral-shaped cochlea in the inner ear. The cochlea is filled with a fluid. Tiny hairs inside the cochlea pick up vibrations in the fluid, and cause nerve signals to be sent to the brain.

DECIBEL SCALE

Sound volume is measured in decibels (dB). The decibel scale is known as a logarithmic scale. The intensity of a sound goes up 10 times for every 10 dB, which means that a sound at 80 dB is ten times as intense as a sound at 70 dB. At 140 dB, the threshold of pain is 100 billion times as intense as the sound of whispering!

10 Breathing

20 Rustling leaves

30 Whispering

40 Refrigerator

RANGE OF SOUNDS

Sound waves have an amplitude and a frequency. The amplitude is the loudness of the sound, while the frequency is its pitch – how high or low it sounds. Pitch is measured in hertz (Hz), which is the number of vibrations per second.

Amplitude
Wavelength (the shorter the wavelength, the higher the frequency)

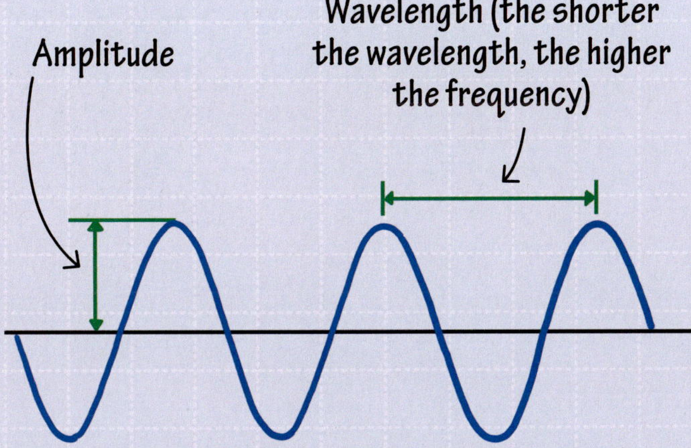

We can detect sounds that range from 20 Hz to 20,000 Hz. Dogs can hear sounds as high as 50,000 Hz. A dog whistle makes a high-pitched sound that dogs can hear but humans cannot.

Distance to right ear
Sound source
Distance to left ear

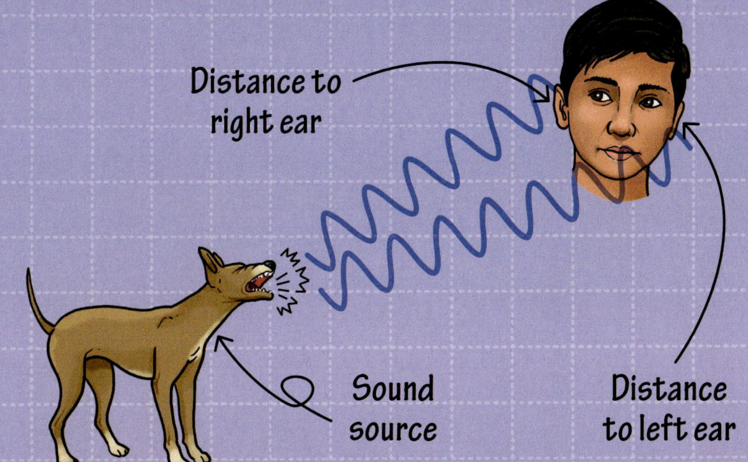

SENSING DIRECTION

Sounds travel through air at a speed of 343 metres per second. The ears are spaced about 20 cm apart. This means that a sound coming from the right will reach the right ear about half a millisecond before it reaches the left ear. The sound will also be slightly louder in the right ear than the left. The brain detects small differences in timing and loudness to work out the direction the sound is coming from.

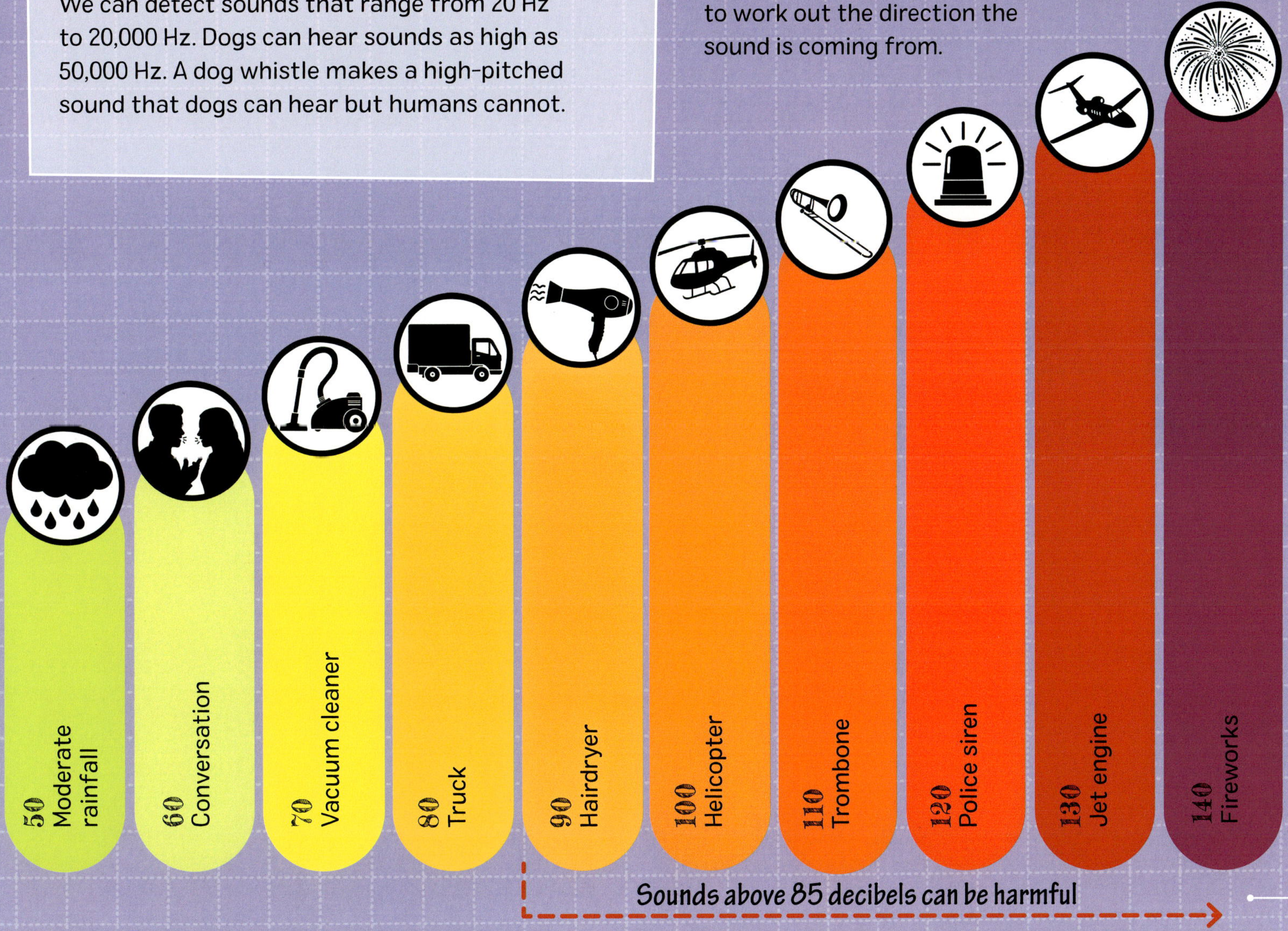

50 Moderate rainfall
60 Conversation
70 Vacuum cleaner
80 Truck
90 Hairdryer
100 Helicopter
110 Trombone
120 Police siren
130 Jet engine
140 Fireworks
Sounds above 85 decibels can be harmful

OTHER SENSES

We often think of five main senses: seeing, hearing, touching, tasting and smelling. However, there are many other senses, including a sense of temperature and a sense of body position.

Merkel's disk detects light pressure.

Skin surface

Meissner's corpuscle detects pressure and low frequency vibrations.

Ruffini corpuscle detects stretch.

Pacinian corpuscle detects high-frequency vibrations.

TOUCH

There are three main kinds of touch receptor in the dermis layer of the skin. Mechanoreceptors sense pressure. Thermoreceptors sense temperature. Pain receptors send out pain signals if the skin is damaged. Pain receptors are found throughout the body.

SENSITIVE FINGERS

The fingertips are packed full of mechanoreceptors. They are also covered in swirls of raised lines, which create your fingerprint. Fingerprints greatly increase the sensitivity of fingers. The ridges of fingerprints magnify the size of tiny vibrations when we run our fingers across a surface, allowing the Pacinian corpuscles to detect them.

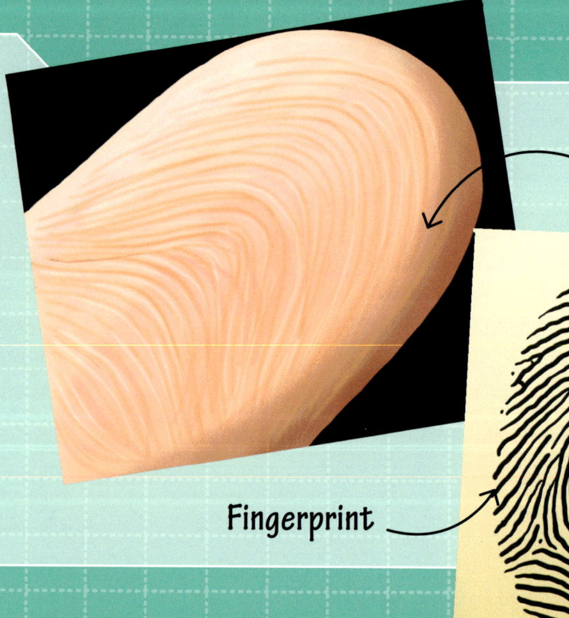

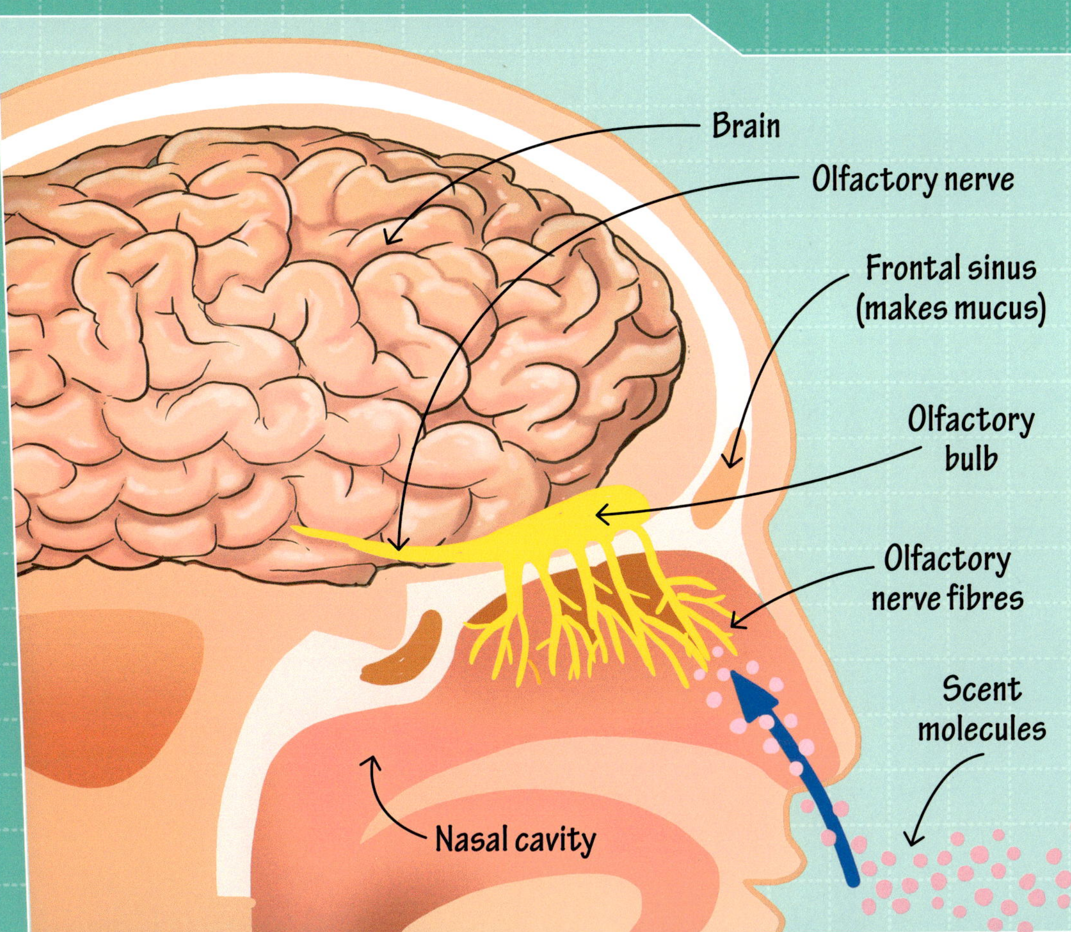

SMELL

Our noses detect tiny amounts of chemicals in the air. Scent particles dissolve in the mucus lining of the nose and are detected by sensors, which send a signal to the brain via the olfactory bulb. The sensors can detect 10,000 different odours.

TASTE

We taste our food using sensors in our mouths called taste buds, which are contained in bumps called papillae. We can detect five kinds of flavour: sweet, sour, salty, bitter and umami (savoury). The full sensation of the flavour of food comes from a combination of its taste and its smell.

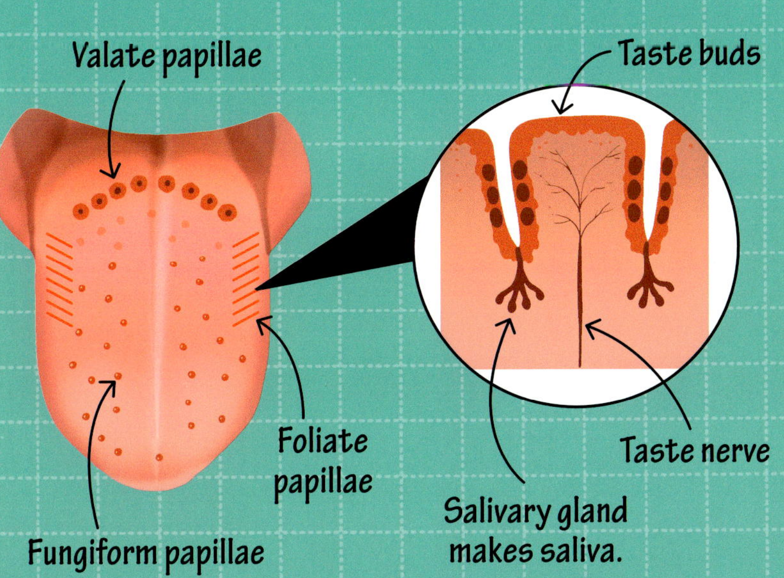

SENSING THE SELF

In addition to sensing the outside world, the body also senses itself. Sensors inside muscles send messages to the brain and spinal cord to say what position each part of the body is in and how it is moving. This is a sense called proprioception.

Standing on one leg with your eyes closed, you rely on proprioception to make small adjustments and stay balanced.

THE DIGESTIVE SYSTEM

When you eat, your food starts on a long journey through your body. It takes up to three days for some kinds of food to pass right through the digestive system.

Epiglottis (stops food from entering the trachea)

Salivary glands

Oesophagus

Trachea (windpipe)

1 MOUTH

Digestion starts in the mouth. When you chew your food, it mixes with saliva, forming into a ball-like mass called a bolus.

2 SWALLOWING

When you swallow the bolus, it moves through the oesophagus into the stomach. Muscles in the walls of the oesophagus contract behind the bolus to push it along.

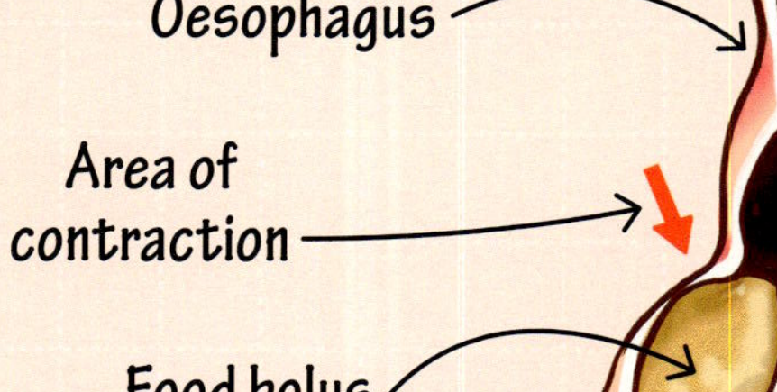

WILLIAM BEAUMONT

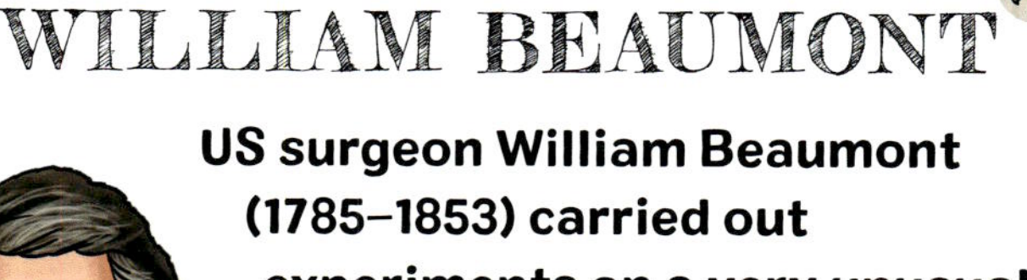

US surgeon William Beaumont (1785–1853) carried out experiments on a very unusual patient – a man with a hole in his stomach. Beaumont was able to extract digestive juices from the man's stomach. He showed that digestion involves chemical reactions between food and acid in the stomach.

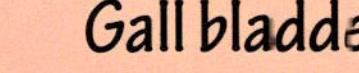

Pancreas

Gall bladder

Liver

3 STOMACH

Food stays in the stomach for between four and six hours. Digestive juices break the food up into smaller pieces to form a liquid called chyme. The digestive juices contain hydrochloric acid, which kills nearly all the bacteria that may be in the food, protecting the body against food poisoning.

4 SMALL INTESTINE

The chyme passes from the stomach into the small intestine—a narrow curled-up tube about 5 metres long. As the chyme passes along the small intestine, nutrients are absorbed into the blood through thousands of finger-like villi. The villi increase the surface area of the small intestine to about 30 square metres.

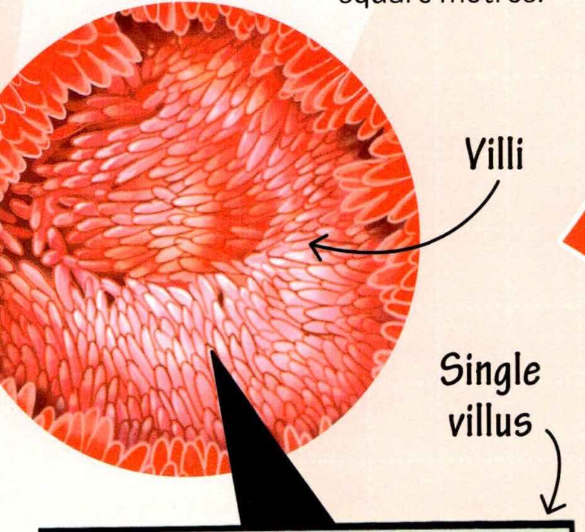

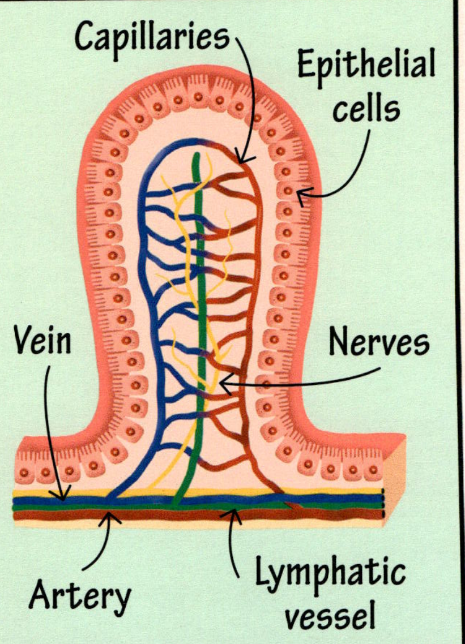

5 LARGE INTESTINE

From the small intestine, the remains of the food pass into the large intestine. The large intestine absorbs water from the remains, leaving the waste product faeces.

6 ANUS

Faeces remains in the large intestine for up to 48 hours before it passes out of the body through the anus.

FILTERING THE BLOOD

Many substances that enter the blood are potentially damaging to the body. The kidneys and liver both filter blood to make sure these substances are removed.

KIDNEYS

The kidneys remove excess water, salts and harmful waste from the blood, making urine. Inside the kidneys, the blood passes through tiny filters called nephrons. The filtered blood leaves the kidneys to travel back to the heart, while the urine is passed from the kidneys to the bladder through the ureters.

Nephrons make urine as they filter the blood. Each kidney contains about 1 million nephrons.

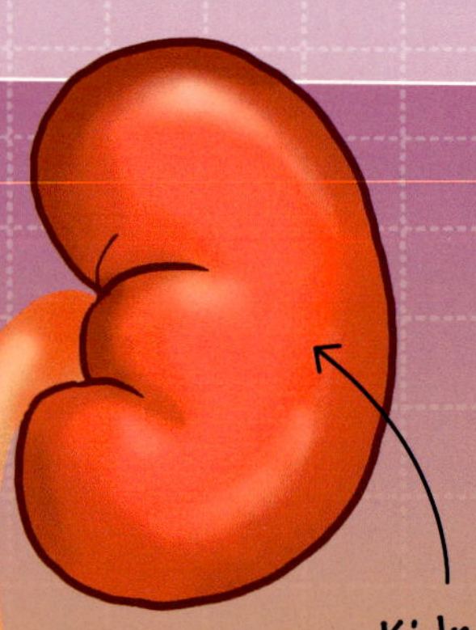

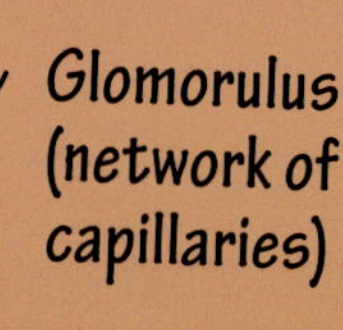

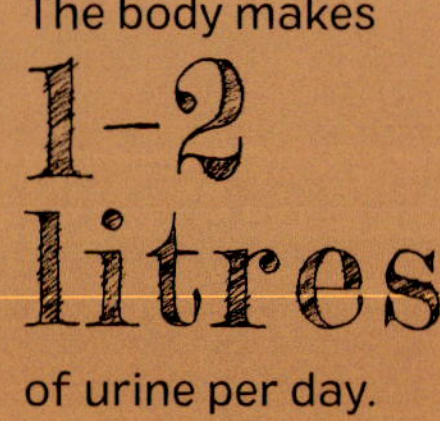

BLADDER

The bladder is a stretchy bag that can hold more than 750 ml of urine. When it is about half-full, stretch sensors on the bladder send a signal to the brain that it is time to go to the toilet and empty the bladder.

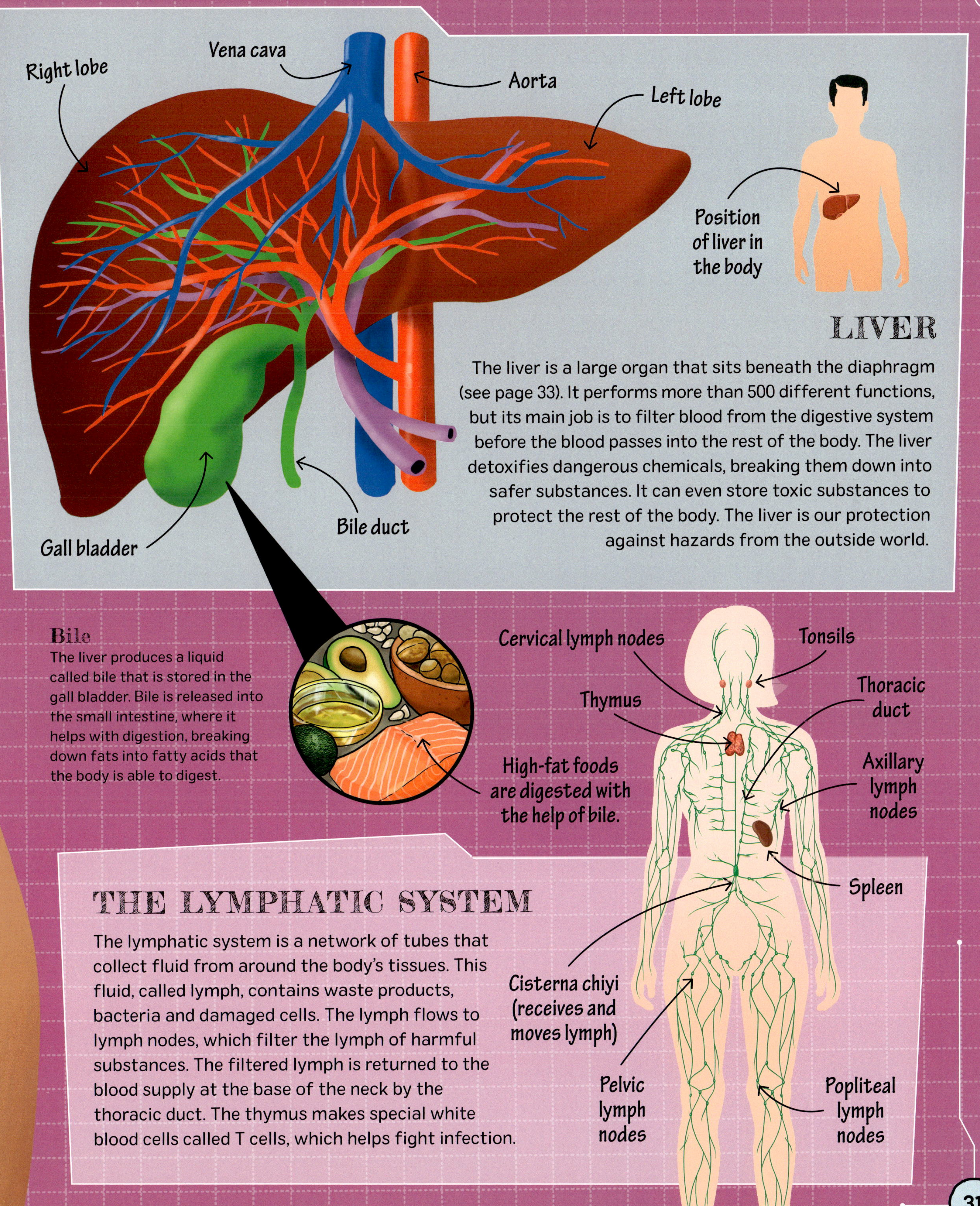

LIVER

The liver is a large organ that sits beneath the diaphragm (see page 33). It performs more than 500 different functions, but its main job is to filter blood from the digestive system before the blood passes into the rest of the body. The liver detoxifies dangerous chemicals, breaking them down into safer substances. It can even store toxic substances to protect the rest of the body. The liver is our protection against hazards from the outside world.

Bile

The liver produces a liquid called bile that is stored in the gall bladder. Bile is released into the small intestine, where it helps with digestion, breaking down fats into fatty acids that the body is able to digest.

THE LYMPHATIC SYSTEM

The lymphatic system is a network of tubes that collect fluid from around the body's tissues. This fluid, called lymph, contains waste products, bacteria and damaged cells. The lymph flows to lymph nodes, which filter the lymph of harmful substances. The filtered lymph is returned to the blood supply at the base of the neck by the thoracic duct. The thymus makes special white blood cells called T cells, which helps fight infection.

THE RESPIRATORY SYSTEM

The respiratory system is responsible for breathing. We breathe in oxygen from the air and breathe out carbon dioxide. We need to keep breathing as it enables vital chemical reactions inside cells.

Nose

Mouth

Trachea

Bronchus

Bronchioles

THE LUNGS

The lungs are two large sacs in your chest. They are filled with hundreds of millions of tiny air sacs called alveoli. The alveoli have very thin walls, which allow oxygen to pass from the air into the blood, and carbon dioxide to pass from the blood into the air.

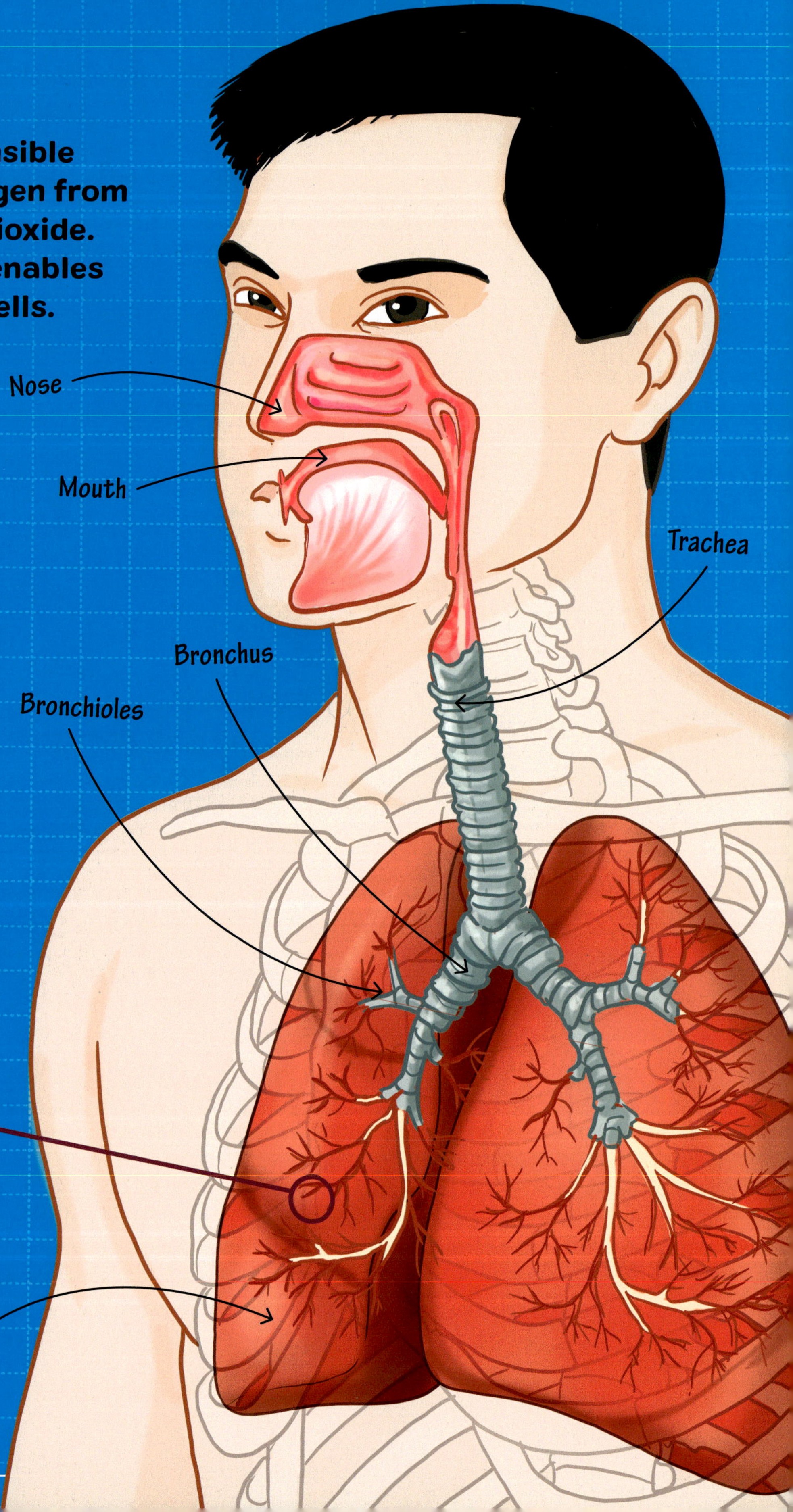

Pulmonary vein carries oxygenated blood.

Alveoli are located at the ends of the bronchioles.

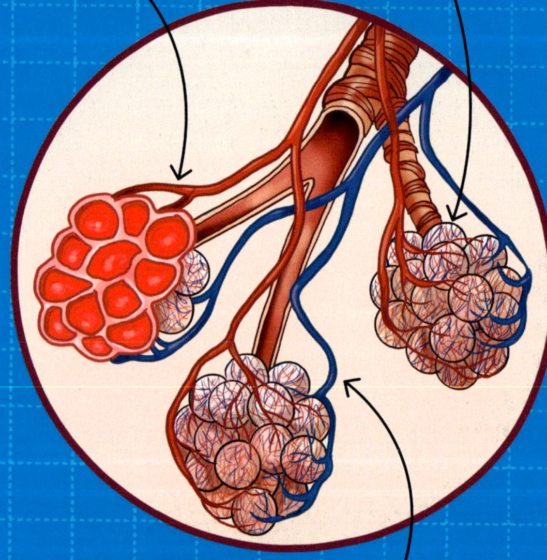

Pulmonary artery carries deoxygenated blood.

Lung

BREATHING

When you breathe in, a muscle underneath the lungs called the diaphragm contracts, pulling it flat, while muscles between the ribs contract to pull the rib cage up. This creates more space within the body for the lungs to expand, sucking air in through trachea from the nose and mouth. When you breathe out, the diaphragm and rib muscles relax. This presses on the lungs, pushing air out through the trachea.

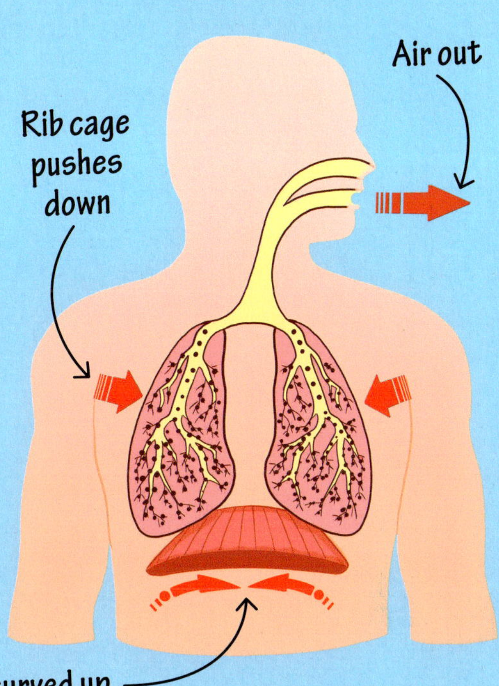

Releasing energy

Respiration is a set of chemical reactions inside cells that release energy from food. Oxygen passes from the blood into the cell, where it combines with sugars to produce the energy-carrying substance ATP (see page 6). This also produces water and carbon dioxide. The carbon dioxide is potentially harmful. It passes back into the blood to be breathed out by the lungs.

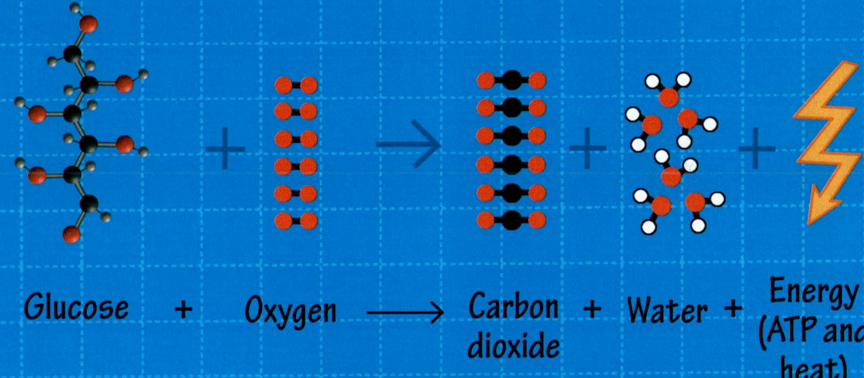

HANS KREBS

British-German biochemist Hans Krebs (1900–1981) discovered the series of chemical reactions that release energy from food during respiration. This is now known as the Krebs cycle. These reactions can also happen in the reverse direction, for instance when plants use the energy of the Sun to make sugars.

THE ENDOCRINE SYSTEM

The endocrine system is made up of a network of glands that produce chemical messengers called hormones. The hormones are released into the bloodstream and reach every cell in the body, producing a wide variety of effects.

Hypothalamus

Pituitary gland

Pineal gland

Brain
There are three glands inside the brain. The hypothalamus and pituitary gland produce a range of hormones that control the production of hormones by other glands. The pineal gland produces hormones that control sleep patterns.

Thyroid
The thyroid gland produces hormones that control the speed at which your cells work.

Thymus
The thymus stimulates the production of T cells, a type of white blood cell that fights disease.

Adrenal glands
These sit above the kidneys. They produce hormones called adrenaline and noradrenaline, which prepare the body for action in dangerous situations.

Pancreas
This organ produces insulin, a hormone that regulates blood sugar levels.

Gonads (testes in males and ovaries in females) These glands produce sex hormones. The testes produce testosterone, which stimulates sperm production and affects body and bone mass. The ovaries produce oestrogen and progesterone, which regulate a woman's reproductive cycle (see page 43). They also produce small amounts of testosterone.

Ovaries (female)

Testes (male)

SLOW AND FAST

Some hormones act on the body very slowly. The growth hormone produced by the pituitary gland causes the body to grow throughout childhood. Growth hormone levels are highest during puberty, when bodies experience a rapid growth spurt.

American Robert Wadlow (1918–1940) had an enlarged pituitary gland that produced too much growth hormone. Wadlow was already as tall as an adult man aged seven, and he was still growing when he died aged 22. Standing 2.72 metres tall, he was the tallest person ever recorded.

Robert Wadlow standing next to his father.

Dorothy Hodgkin
British chemist Dorothy Crowfoot Hodgkin (1910–1994) worked out the three-dimensional structure of many important molecules in the body, including the hormone insulin. Her discovery enabled the mass-production of insulin for the treatment of diabetes.

Some hormones act very quickly. Adrenaline produces a range of changes in the body within just a few seconds. These changes prepare the body for immediate action.

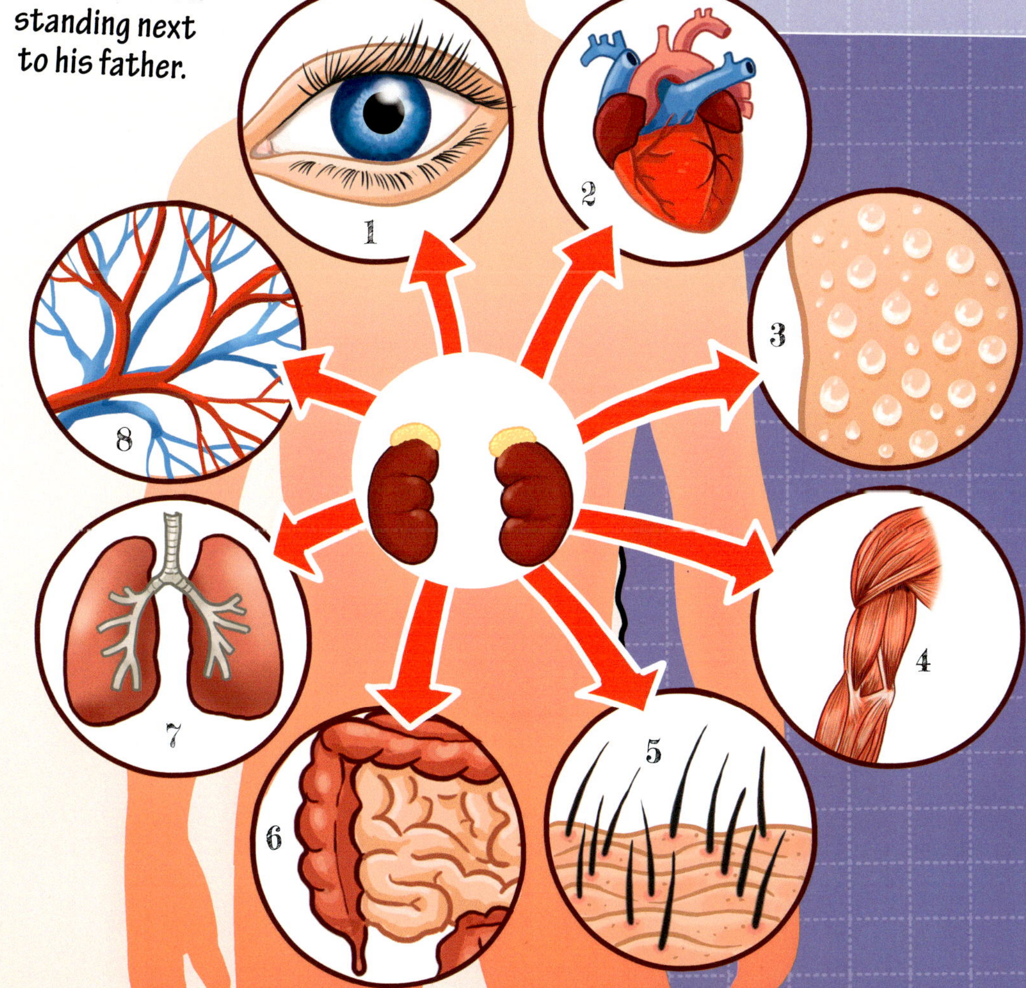

1 Pupils of the eye widen
2 Heart rate increases
3 Skin sweats
4 Blood is sent to muscles
5 Hairs stand on end
6 Digestion slows, causing butterflies in the stomach
7 Breathing increases
8 Blood pressure goes up

HEALING THE BODY

A white blood cell can attack many pathogens at once by extending out thin arms called pseudopodia.

When you are injured or get sick, your body has a number of ways to make you better.

WHITE BLOOD CELLS

White blood cells have the job of protecting the body from infectious diseases. White blood cells called phagocytes identify and destroy pathogens, which are harmful viruses, bacteria or other microorganisms. White blood cells 'eat' pathogens in a process called phagocytosis.

BLOOD CLOTS

When the wall of a blood vessel is broken, platelets in the blood are called into action. They change shape from round to spiny and stick to each other across the gap. The platelets combine with proteins in the blood to form a substance called fibrin. Strands of fibrin form a net, which traps more platelets and red blood cells to plug the gap. This blood clot protects the tissues underneath while they repair themselves.

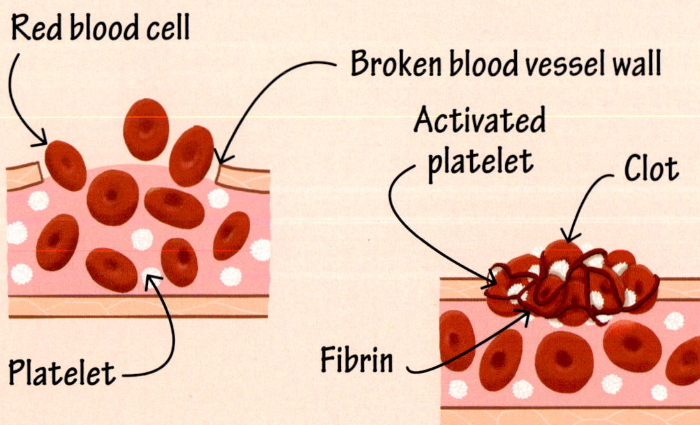

LOUIS PASTEUR

French chemist Louis Pasteur (1822–1895) developed the germ theory of disease. He showed that diseases can be spread by invisible microbes in the air. Inspired by Pasteur's work, surgeons started to sterilise wounds during surgery to stop them from becoming infected.

FIRST LINE OF DEFENCE

The best way to stay healthy is to avoid taking in harmful substances in the first place. The skin forms a barrier to most invaders. Tears keep the eyes moist and also attack and kill germs. Mucus in your nose traps particles in the air so that they can be swallowed and dealt with by the strong acid in the stomach. Sneezing also clears the nose of unwanted irritants. Washing your hands can help to stop germs spreading.

REPAIRING BONES

When a bone fractures, or breaks, it can heal itself. A cast will stop the bone from moving whilst it heals. There are three stages to the healing process.

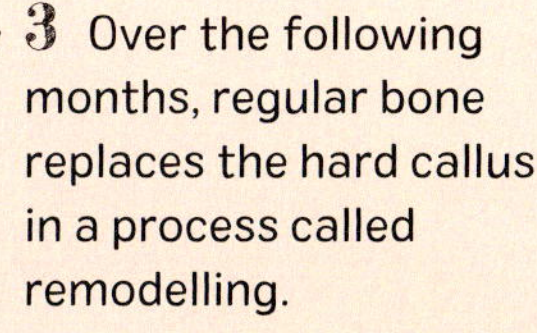

1 A blood clot, or haematoma, forms around the fracture.

2 After a few days, a type of soft bone called callus replaces the blood clot. The callus gradually hardens over the next few weeks.

3 Over the following months, regular bone replaces the hard callus in a process called remodelling.

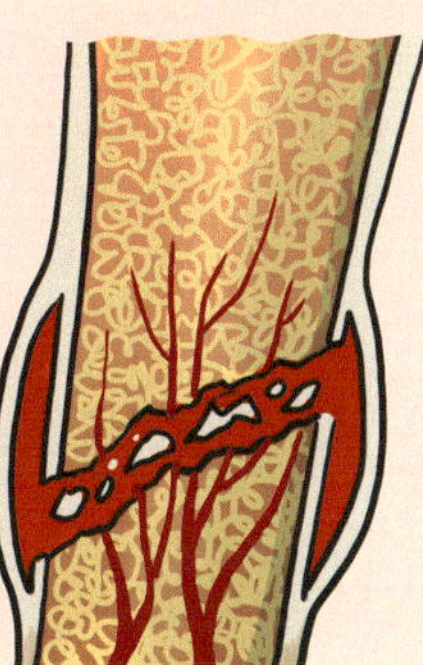

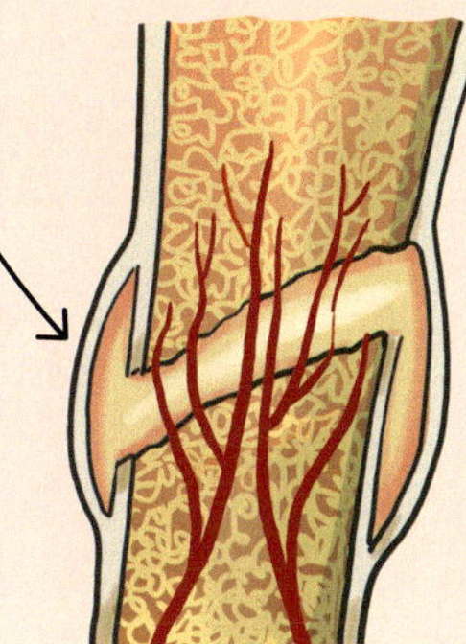

REPRODUCTION

Reproduction starts when a man's sperm fertilises a woman's egg inside the woman's fallopian tube. This creates a single-celled zygote. The zygote starts to divide to form a small bundle of cells called a blastocyst.

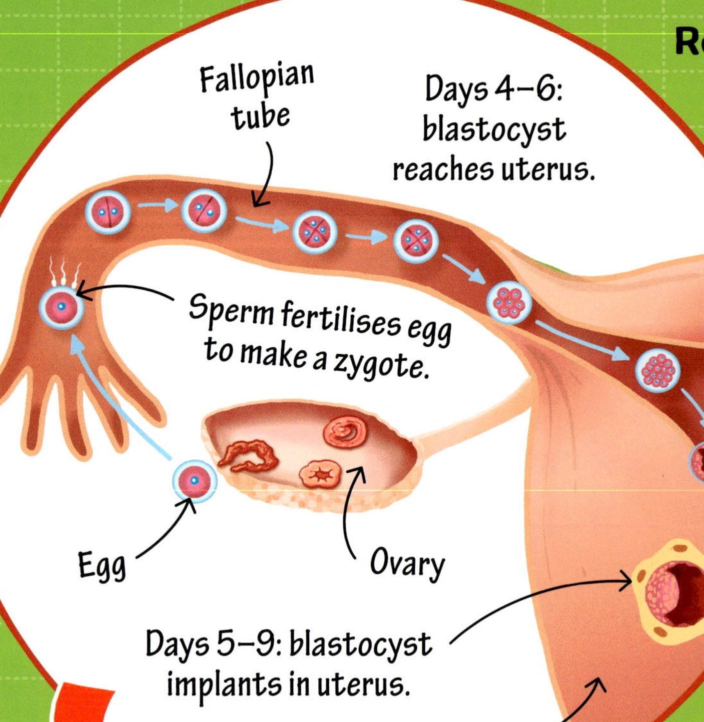

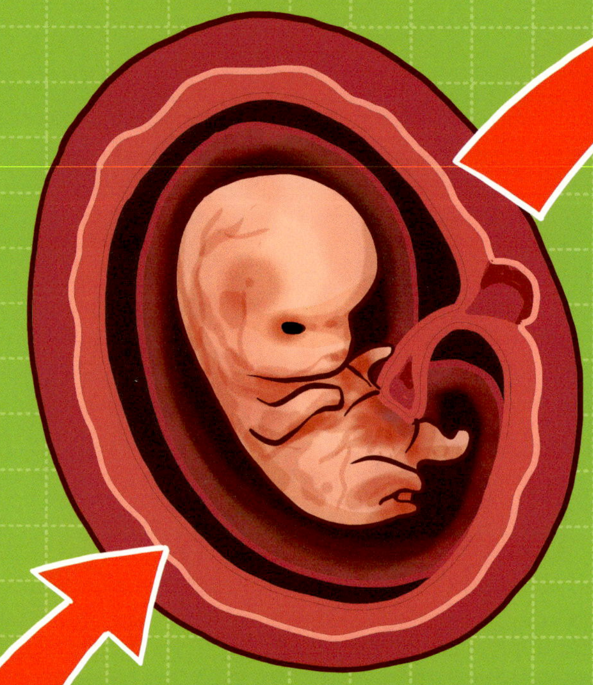

Towards the womb

In the first week after fertilisation, the blastocyst moves down the fallopian tube to the uterus, or womb. It burrows into the soft lining of the uterus. At this stage, it is only 0.2 mm in diameter. Safely embedded in the uterus, the dividing cells start to become different from one another and an embryo develops.

8 weeks

The arms and legs have started growing, and it is recognisably a human shape. It is now called a foetus.

THE DEVELOPING FOETUS

The embryo develops rapidly in the uterus, taking nutrients from the mother's blood. After a few weeks, it starts to take human shape and is known as a foetus.

4 weeks

The embryo's internal organs have started to develop. It is about the size of a pea.

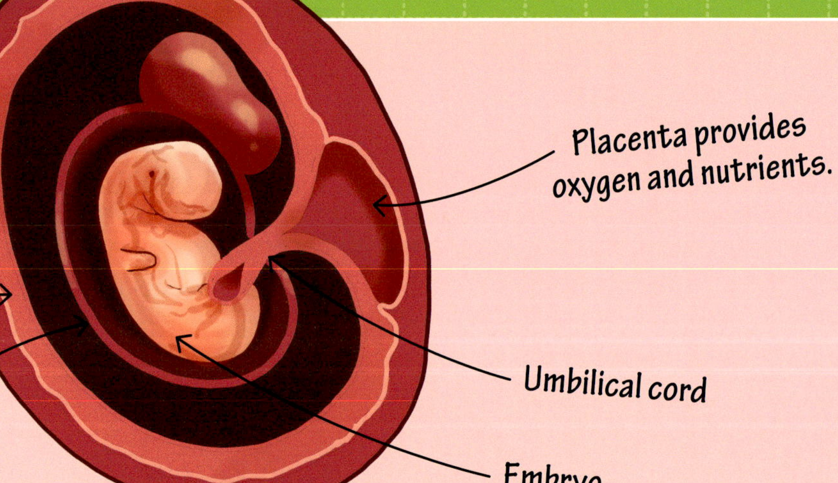

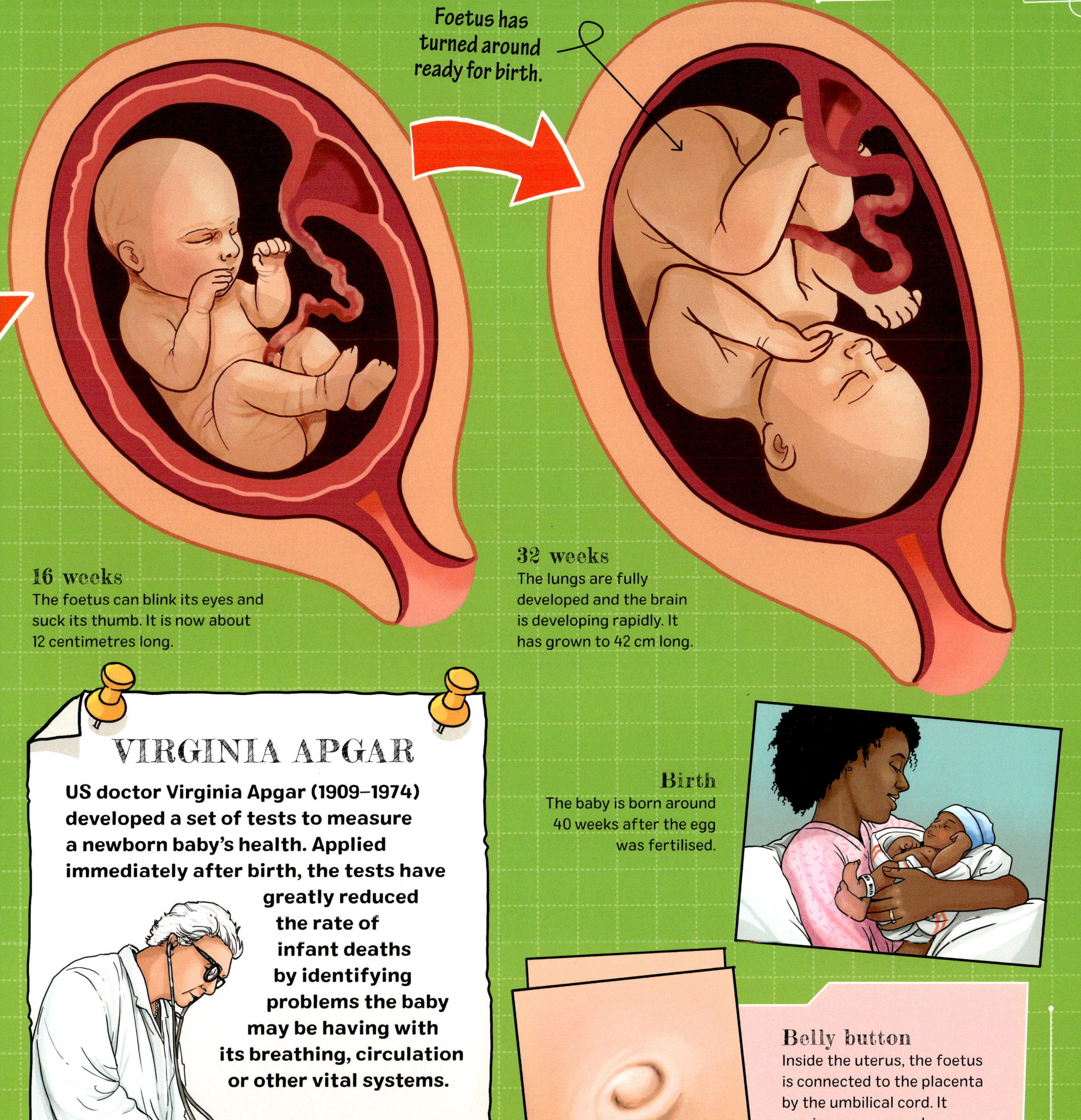

16 weeks
The foetus can blink its eyes and suck its thumb. It is now about 12 centimetres long.

32 weeks
The lungs are fully developed and the brain is developing rapidly. It has grown to 42 cm long.

VIRGINIA APGAR

US doctor Virginia Apgar (1909–1974) developed a set of tests to measure a newborn baby's health. Applied immediately after birth, the tests have greatly reduced the rate of infant deaths by identifying problems the baby may be having with its breathing, circulation or other vital systems.

Birth
The baby is born around 40 weeks after the egg was fertilised.

Belly button
Inside the uterus, the foetus is connected to the placenta by the umbilical cord. It receives oxygen and nutrients from the mother's blood via the placenta. When the baby is born, the umbilical cord is cut, leaving behind a belly button.

THE CODE FOR LIFE

With the exception of red blood, hair and nail cells, each of our cells contains the complete instructions for how to make a body. These instructions take the form of 23 pairs of chromosomes inside the cell nucleus.

Discovering the double-helix

The double-helix structure of DNA was discovered in 1953 by James Watson (born 1928) and Francis Crick (1916–2004), using X-ray images produced by their colleagues Rosalind Franklin, Raymond Gosling and Maurice Wilkins. The discovery helped to solve the mystery as to how DNA codes for life.

DNA

A chromosome is made of a single molecule of deoxyribonucleic acid (DNA). The DNA molecule is a double-helix with two strands that wind around one another. The strands are connected to one another by a series of up to 300 million base pairs.

Sense strand

Guanine (G) pairs with cytosine

Cytosine (C) pairs with guanine

Thymine (T) pairs with adenine

Adenine (A) pairs with thymine

Antisense strand

BASE PAIRS

Bases are formed from four different chemicals: guanine (G), cytosine (C), thymine (T) and adenine (A). Guanine on one strand always pairs with cytosine on the other strand, while thymine always pairs with adenine. Each base pair takes one of four values, read along the sense strand: G, C, T or A.

CODONS

Groups of three base pairs are called codons. Each codon can take one of 64 different values. The codons code for chemicals called amino acids, plus the instructions START and STOP. For example, the codon GAG codes for the amino acid glutamate. Amino acids join together to form larger molecules called proteins, which are the building blocks of our bodies. Protein molecules are made of chains of up to 2,000 amino acids.

Sense strand

C C C

T C A

G A G

GENES

The main job of DNA is to code for the creation of proteins. The thousands of proteins in the human body are all made using combinations of the same 20 amino acids. Groups of codons code for specific proteins. These groups of codons are called genes.

Protein molecule

GENETIC INHERITANCE

A human cell contains about 25,000 genes. We inherit roughly half of our genes from each of our parents. This means that we share 50 per cent of our genes with our parents and our siblings. These are our closest relatives, and we sometimes look a lot like them. Identical twins grow from the same fertilised egg. They share 100 per cent of their genes with one another.

A COMMON ANCESTOR

All living things contain DNA, and the DNA of all life on Earth codes for amino acids in exactly the same way. This is because we share a common ancestor from billions of years ago. Every living thing on Earth is related to every other living thing!

GROWING UP

It takes many years for a human to grow from a baby to an adult. Throughout this period, the body undergoes huge changes and the brain learns countless new skills.

BABIES

A newborn baby is completely dependent on its parents. However, the baby is learning all the time. In the first few months, the baby will learn to focus its eyes and start exploring the world around it.

INFANCY AND CHILDHOOD

Over the first couple of years of life, an infant learns how to walk and how to speak. In early childhood, they will learn complex physical skills such as riding a bike and mental skills such as reading.

PUBERTY

Puberty is a period of rapid change as a child's body takes on an adult shape.

Girls

In girls, puberty commonly starts around age 10-11. The girl's breasts start to grow and she undergoes a growth spurt. The hips widen and hair grows in the pubic area. About 2 years after the start of puberty, a girl's periods start. These are part of the menstrual cycle, a monthly series of changes in an adult woman's body.

Boys

Puberty normally starts about a year later for boys than girls. The boy's penis and testes grow larger and he undergoes a growth spurt. The chest and shoulders become broader, and hair grows in the pubic area. About 2 years after the start of puberty, a boy's voice breaks. This happens because the voice box, or larynx, becomes larger.

CLUMSY TEENS

During puberty, the brain struggles to keep up with the rapid changes that are happening in the body. During a growth spurt, the brain has to relearn how to control a different, bigger body, and for a while a teenager may become clumsy. The clumsiness goes away once the growth spurt has ended.

DEVELOPING BRAIN

Our brains continue to develop until our mid-20s, but the first year of life sees the most rapid changes. The brain of a newborn baby rapidly makes new synapses, and the brain of a one-year-old has twice as many connections as an adult brain. This is a period of rapid learning. Many of these connections disappear through childhood in a process called synaptic pruning. Only the pathways through the brain that prove useful are kept.

BIONIC BODIES

When our bodies stop working properly or when we lose a body part, we quickly realise how easily bodies can go wrong. In recent years, scientists have made amazing advances in producing replacement body parts.

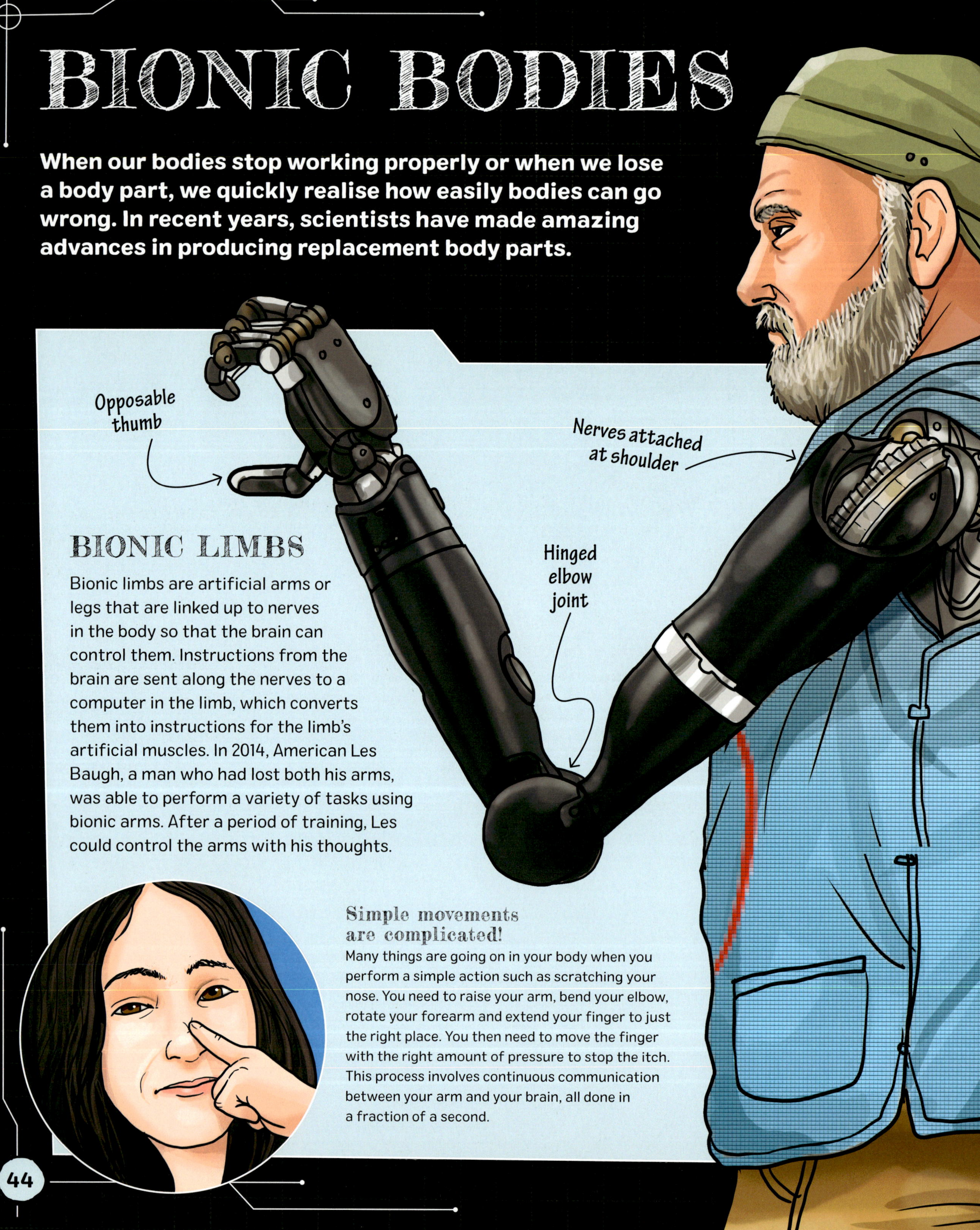

BIONIC LIMBS

Bionic limbs are artificial arms or legs that are linked up to nerves in the body so that the brain can control them. Instructions from the brain are sent along the nerves to a computer in the limb, which converts them into instructions for the limb's artificial muscles. In 2014, American Les Baugh, a man who had lost both his arms, was able to perform a variety of tasks using bionic arms. After a period of training, Les could control the arms with his thoughts.

Simple movements are complicated!

Many things are going on in your body when you perform a simple action such as scratching your nose. You need to raise your arm, bend your elbow, rotate your forearm and extend your finger to just the right place. You then need to move the finger with the right amount of pressure to stop the itch. This process involves continuous communication between your arm and your brain, all done in a fraction of a second.

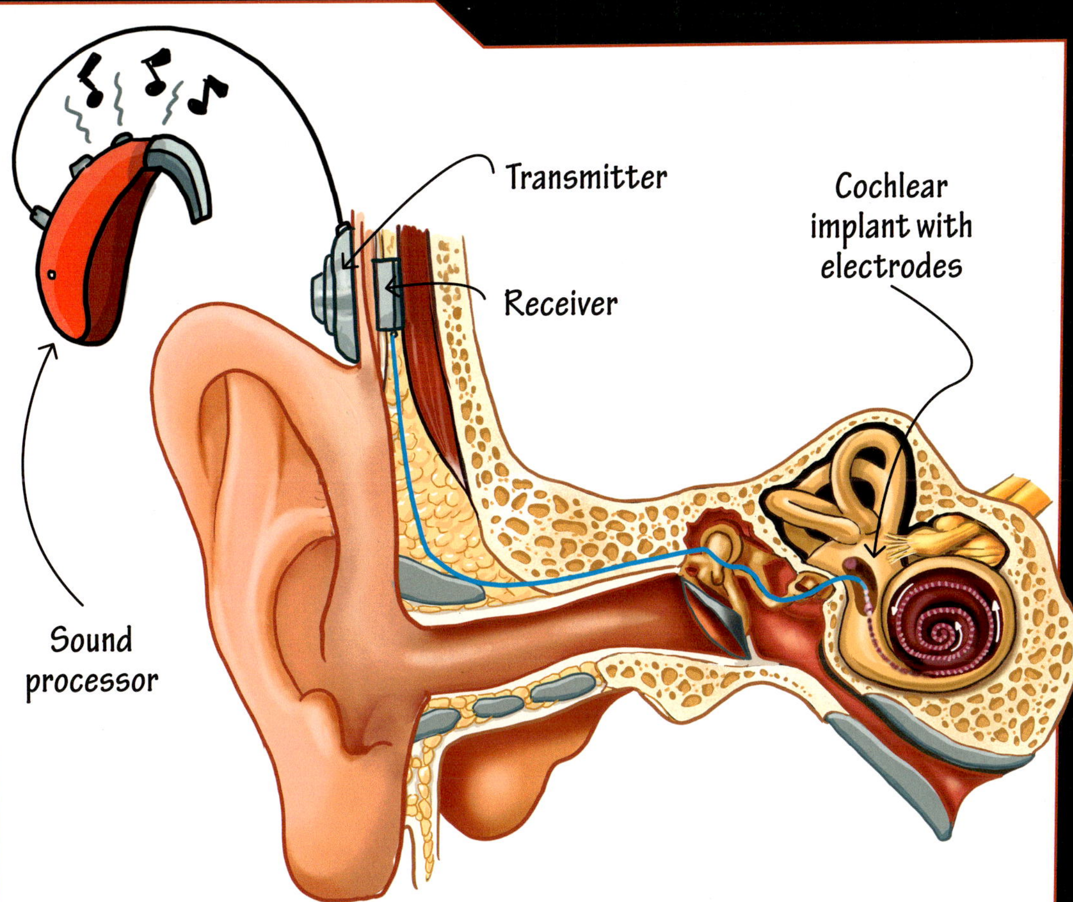

Bionic touch

Communication between brain and limb works both ways. The brain tells the limb how to move, but the limb also sends back crucial information such as the sense of touch. This is how you know how hard to scratch an itch. The next generation of bionic limbs will have pressure sensors fitted to them. These sensors will be connected to the sensory cortex, the part of the brain that processes the senses.

BIONIC EARS

Cochlear implants are hearing aids that can give a sense of hearing to someone who is completely deaf. A microphone placed near the ear picks up sounds and radios them to a receiver implanted in the cochlea. The receiver converts the sounds into electrical signals that are passed directly to the auditory nerve, which sends them to the brain.

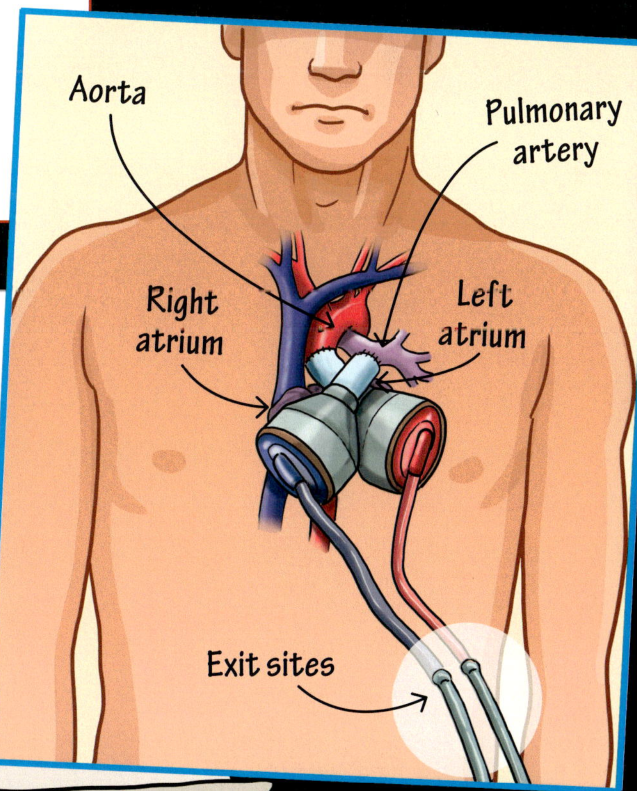

BIONIC HEARTS

Patients with failing hearts may be fitted with a total artificial heart (TAH) while they await a heart transplant. The TAH replaces the heart's two lower chambers, the ventricles, which pump blood through the body. It is connected to an electric driver, which can be carried around in a bag.

GLOSSARY

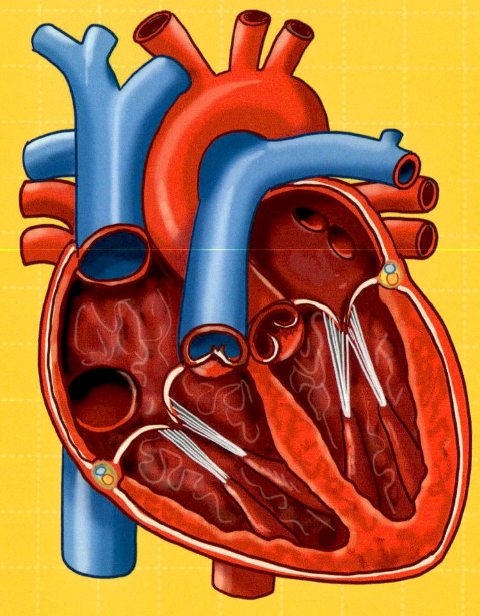

Artery
A blood vessel that carries blood away from the heart.

Atria
(singular atrium) The two top chambers of the heart into which blood enters from the veins.

Bacteria
Simple single-celled organisms. Our bodies are home to trillions of bacteria. Some make us ill, while others help to perform important jobs such as digestion.

Capillaries
Tiny blood vessels with thin walls that allow oxygen and nutrients to pass into cells from the blood and waste products to pass into the blood from the cells.

Cell
The smallest working unit of a body. A human body is made of about 30 trillion cells.

Chromosome
A long molecule of DNA (deoxyribonucleic acid) that contains genetic information. A cell nucleus contains 46 chromosomes.

Fungus
A group of organisms that includes yeast, mould and mushrooms. Various kinds of fungus can infect human bodies.

Gene
A section of a chromosome that contains a particular set of information, such as the instructions to make a protein.

Homeostasis
The maintenance of a healthy internal balance within a body, an organ or an individual cell.

Hormone
A chemical that is released into the blood to control the actions of cells or organs.

Joint
A place at which two bones meet. Some joints fix bones in place, while others allow certain kinds of movement.

Mitochondria
(singular mitochondrion) Structures inside cells that release energy.

Muscle
A body tissue that can contract. Muscles work together to move body parts.

Neuron
Also called a nerve cell, a type of cell that sends and receives electrical messages.

Nucleus
A structure with a membrane inside cells that contains the cell's chromosomes.

Organ
A part of the body made of a number of tissues that work together to perform a particular job or set of jobs.

Photoreceptors
Cells in the eye that sense light. Rods sense colour, while cones allow us to see in black-and-white in low light.

Platelets
Small fragments of cells in the blood that help the blood to clot.

Proprioception
A sense that allows us to keep track of the positions of different parts of our bodies.

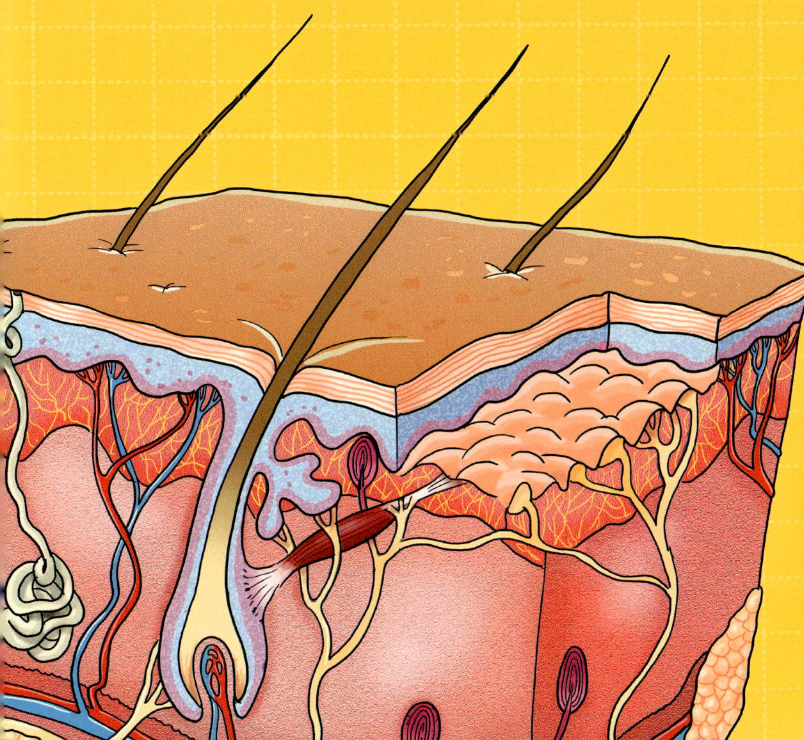

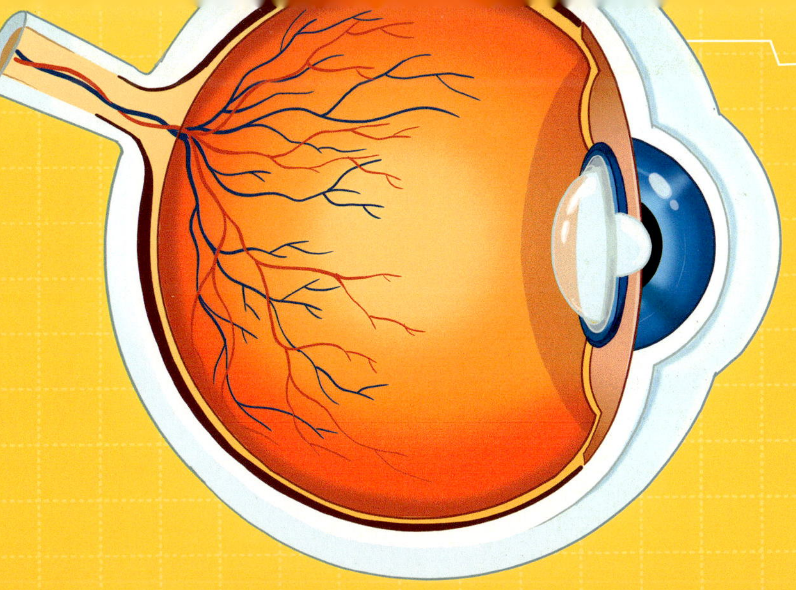

Synapse
A tiny gap across which two neurons communicate with one another.

Tendon
A strong, flexible cord that connects muscles to bones.

Tissue
A group of similar cells that perform a particular job in the body.

Trachea
Also called the windpipe, a tube that carries air between the lungs and the mouth.

Uterus
Also called the womb, the organ in a woman's body inside which a foetus grows and develops.

Vein
A blood vessel that carries blood towards the heart.

Ventricles
The two lower chambers of the heart, which forcefully pump blood into the arteries.

INDEX